Sherman Williams, pastor of Redwood Chapel Community Church since 1961.

More than 700 people attended Sunday School on this particular Sunday during a contest in March 1967. The total number present on the last Sunday of the contest was 862. The Sunday School now averages that number or more every Sunday.

Rev. Winston Miller,
Minister of Christian
Education since 1971.

Sunday School enthusiasm resulted in an attendance of over
1100 on Demonstration Day, 1974, a special promotional effort.

The nursery, presided over by "Grandma Doty," is designed to provide an atmosphere of love and acceptance, as well as teaching.

Children's Church provides worship services for children on their level of understanding, and includes their participation.

Personal attention is a keynote of the Sunday School, and men take part in teaching even the smallest boys and girls.

Unique "Circle Classes" for adults have led to heightened interest and attendance.

Christian Service Brigade for boys and Pioneer Girls are agencies of the local church for evangelism and training.

Don Larmour, Redwood's Minister of Youth, makes Bible study, discipleship, and Christian leadership the main emphases of his program.

Blacking out bus windows to keep destinations a mystery is part of the preparation for the annual Halloween Party which climaxes with hundreds of high schoolers hearing the Gospel.

The Chapel Choir, including special singing groups, the Revised Edition and Chapel Singers.

The Revised Edition, formed specifically for the television outreach ministry.

The Junior Choir, for grades four, five, and six, helps lead worship periodically.

Touring groups have travelled as far away as Canada to present the Good News in song and testimony.

Joseph Linn, Minister of Music, is a composer, arranger, and director with numerous recording credits.

Neal Doty, Associate Pastor of Redwood Church, is also host and producer of "Sunday Nite Sing," a radio/TV musical variety program.

"Sunday Nite Sing" is produced before a live audience in the church sanctuary.

Master Control at Redwood Teleproductions is manned by a volunteer staff.

Sunday services at Redwood are televised live to the community on Cable Channel 12, and taped for later rebroadcast on the channel.

The second branch church founded by people from Redwood Chapel is in Fremont, Calif. The work started with 60 in attendance, grew by 300% the first year.

Redwood Christian School started with 75 students, now numbers over 500, with two elementary and one high school campus.

pattern for a total Church

**Sherman Williams
and his staff
share ways any church can grow**

Bernard Palmer

VICTOR BOOKS

a division of SP Publications, Inc.

WHEATON, ILLINOIS 60187

Library of Congress Catalog Card Number: 75-8026
ISBN: 0-88207-717-1

© 1975 by SP Publications, Inc. World rights reserved
Printed in the United States of America

VICTOR BOOKS
A division of SP Publications, Inc.
P.O. Box 1825 • Wheaton, Ill. 60187

Contents

Foreword

The quick smile, gracious spirit, and solid commitment of Sherman Williams was deeply impressed upon my mind long before I ever heard of Redwood Chapel Community Church. I'm not surprised, therefore, at what has happened there under his leadership. Sherm (as he is known by all his friends) understands the importance of getting people together and working toward common objectives. Furthermore, he knows how to do it.

As a former pastor, I deeply appreciate the emphasis at Redwood Chapel on a total church program, which results in a concern for the entire family. Too many evangelical churches are guilty of developing programs which tend to dissect the family or which minister effectively to only one or two age levels within the family. It seems to me the commitment of Redwood Chapel to reach and minister to *all* members of the family is a goal every church would do well to adopt.

The story of Redwood Chapel is also an account of Pastor Williams' expertise in delegating responsibility to both his paid staff and lay leaders. Unfortunately, many pastors still haven't learned they can't do all the work. The wise pastor will strive to equip the saints for their work of ministry (Eph. 4:11-12).

I commend this book to every pastor and church leader. It is brimful of tested and proven ideas which can help any church develop a total church program.

Dr. Billy A. Melvin
Executive Director
National Association of Evangelicals

21

Preface

There are a number of super churches in evangelical circles across America today. Most of them are pastored by men of great stature and personal magnetism. They attract huge crowds and have built vast organizations. Usually they have the necessary money and staff to carry out successfully any project they select. It is fascinating to read about such churches and their accomplishments. Seldom, however, can their methods be appropriated by pastors with small staffs and limited financial resources.

Redwood Chapel Community Church in Castro Valley, Calif. does not fall into that category. Pastor Sherman Williams is an excellent Bible teacher and speaker and an able administrator. Still, he would be the first to disclaim the statement that what has been done at the church he serves is beyond the reach of others.

The program he and his staff have put together is diversified and imaginative, designed to meet the needs of their people and to reach the lost in the community. Their methods closely follow those principles so carefully worked out by capable Christian educators and authorities on church growth, principles that have been proved over a number of years in a variety of churches under different situations in all parts of the country.

They have worked at Redwood Chapel. Properly adapted to your special situation, they will work for you.

Bernard Palmer

Sherman Williams immediately strikes you as a man of action and energy. Whether in the pulpit or behind the desk, words pour from him in short, quick phrases, punctuated with gestures. He is excited about the Lord, and about serving Him. His eyes sparkle with the enthusiasm of a used car salesman, but the smile is genuine and quick. There is a pastor's heart, too, expressed in the gentleness of the eyes.

Though he is not physically a large man, a dynamic is apparent in his walk and gestures. It is characteristic of him that when he played tennis in high school and college, he developed a special serve that maximized his height, and took opponents off guard with its power. He was and is "on the stretch," and that phrase comes often from his lips as he urges his men to follow his example. There is about him a conservatism with flair—a controlled energy that gets things done.

Neal Doty
Associate Pastor
Redwood Chapel Community Church

1

Evaluating Redwood Chapel

Sherman Williams was happy and contented in his work with a Midwestern publisher of Sunday School materials back in 1961. He had received Christ as his Saviour at the age of eight. As a young man, he had been ordained by the Wheaton Bible Church (Wheaton, Ill.). After serving an interdenominational church for 10 years, he felt God was calling him to leave the pastorate for a wider avenue of service as director of the Christian Education Extension Department of Scripture Press Publications. In this role, he enjoyed getting around the country, visiting different churches, meeting pastors, and presenting workshops at Sunday School conventions.

It was gratifying to be able to suggest to other men ways of doing things that would make their ministry more effective. He especially enjoyed going back a couple of years later to see the fruit of his suggestions. It gave him a sense of accomplishment that added real purpose to his work and helped him feel he was in God's will.

In his position he had the privilege of teaching both laymen and pastors, but he learned from them as well. His notebook bulged with new methods and ideas garnered in his travels. These were the work of other men who had found an answer to a particular need or situation in their churches. Other ideas were his own, prompted by something someone else was doing, or failures he thought could have been avoided with different approaches.

Now, at the age of 43, a nagging uneasiness had taken hold of him. At first he brushed it aside, but it came back again and again until he could no longer ignore it. He said nothing to his wife and family at the time but began to realize that God might be calling him from his present job back to his first love, pastoring a church.

Then an inquiry came from the Redwood Chapel Community Church in Castro Valley, Calif. Would he consider coming to speak at their church? They were looking for a pastor and he had been highly recommended to them.

At first he wasn't sure what he should do. He didn't want to leave his work and move to California unless he was sure God was leading him.

"No man could ask for a more rewarding job than I have," he confided to his wife, Ruth,* "but my heart is in the pastorate and I've got all these ideas about developing an effective church that I've picked up since I came here to work. I'm beginning to believe that God wants me to try them out."

---

* Sherman and Ruth Williams, who were married May 4, 1940, have four children. Sharon (Mrs. Martin Erickson) lives with her husband and two sons in Ecuador, where they are missionaries with the World Radio Missionary Fellowship; Sherman III, who is married and has a daughter and a son, is pastor of Fremont (Calif.) Community Church; Connie (Mrs. Scott Snyder) serves as her brother's secretary; and Merilee (Mrs. Kenneth Strom) lives in Fullerton, Calif. with her husband and son.

A Typical, Comfortable Church

On the surface, Castro Valley did not seem to be the sort of place a knowledgeable person would choose to try new ideas. People living there were older, on the average, than in some of the neighboring towns where it didn't cost quite so much to live. Many were executives and professional people, given to weighing matters carefully and moving with caution. The community was affluent, and conservative both politically and in life-style.

Williams knew what the people in this Oakland suburb were like and had no reason to believe they would have a different attitude toward new ideas in their church than they would in other areas of their lives.

The interdenominational Redwood Chapel was rather typical of a thousand other churches of similar size. Organized in 1953 by a small group of solid, devout men and women, the congregation had grown at a comfortable rate. Being without a pastor for a few months had reduced their numbers somewhat—to about 220 in Sunday School and an average of 250 in the morning worship service. They weren't a large group, but there were churches in the area that had been around a lot longer than they had and were considerably smaller. In those days most Christians accepted as fact the idea that a church where the Gospel is preached isn't going to attract crowds of people.

Starting with nothing, the congregation now had facilities adequate for its size; they were able to meet their annual budget of $53,000 without difficulty, and they were growing spiritually. In addition to Sunday School, they had a youth work, a women's missionary society, and a full complement of boards, committees, and programs. The founding pastor, Dr. Paul Gaston, who had just resigned to take another charge, was sound doctrinally and forceful in the pulpit.

Redwood Chapel sought out Sherman Williams convinced he would build on the foundation that had been laid. He was an effective speaker,* as spiritually sound as his predecessor. He would challenge believers to godly living and be used to convict nonbelievers of sin.

The congregation at the Redwood Chapel had the same concern for those who were outside of Christ that was typical of the average evangelical church in the early '60s. They wanted the lost to come to their Saviour, and at every prayer meeting someone was sure to petition God to draw unbelievers to the church where they could hear the Gospel.

If the results were less than spectacular, they were typical of a day when most felt that inviting others to attend their church was the fulfillment of their responsibility to witness.

Williams was greatly impressed by many of the people he met at the church. They had a deep concern for reaching out into the community, though they perhaps had not done enough of it. Even the members lacking in such vision were, for the most part, strong in their faith and in their love for the church.

"Some of the people might be a bit slow to accept new ideas," Sherman explained to his family when he told them of his decision. "I couldn't tell about that, for sure. But they are the kind who'll get behind their pastor and give him the support he needs. I'm convinced they'll see that things get done."

The Vision of a Total Program

Williams resigned his position at Scripture Press and with great expectancy moved to California to take a pastorate once more. He knew little about Redwood Chapel or the way it

---

* Pastor Williams has served as a speaker, both before his ministry at Redwood Chapel began and since, in Bible conferences, pastors' seminars, and in scores of national and regional Sunday School conventions across the U.S., Canada, England, and the Orient.

was organized and operated. From his business travels, however, he was well acquainted with the difficulties and problems faced by the average congregation.

He had long since learned that a successful local church had to have a *total program* that was well balanced and effective. It wasn't enough to have a good Sunday School at the expense of everything else, or to simply major in youth work or visitation. The entire ministry had to be well organized, balanced, and strong—a total church program.

Dr. W. A. Criswell of the First Baptist Church in Dallas, Texas often says, "In our church we try to have something for everybody." With that approach, Sherm Williams agrees.

But "something for everybody" could not be achieved hastily, or by inaugurating programs to meet certain needs without attempting to see their effects on the total ministry of the church. Williams was acquainted with congregations where the full force of their efforts was dissipated by rushing into one program or another without weighing the effects on the rest of the ministry. He was determined not to make that mistake. If he moved in the wrong direction he would create more problems than he solved.

"Our first job," he told his wife, "is to get the people to analyze what they've been doing in every department of the church. With that information we can set up goals so we can evaluate our effectiveness against them. We can establish some long-range plans and standards and priorities."

Those ideas were not new to Ruth Williams. She had heard them many times from her husband. They were so elementary she wondered why all churches didn't use them. A congregation had only to find out exactly what was being done in every department and evaluate its effectiveness. That would tell them whether to leave the program as it was or to make changes. They could also see if there were blind spots in their programs—holes that needed filling if they were going to have a well-balanced ministry. It was simple and obvious, yet she knew that too few took the time to evaluate, and then to develop a long-range program of Christian education that included every facet of spiritual life-building.

The Evaluation Sessions

Sherman Williams' first act, once the confusion of moving was over, was to call the chairmen of the various boards together. He asked if they would set up a series of regular meetings with him so they could begin to explore the church program at the Chapel and see how well the various departments were functioning.

"I'd like to meet with you every Monday night for awhile," he told them, "so we can find out exactly what the church is doing and how well we're doing it."

They were somewhat surprised by the approach he was taking. Why not save his time and theirs by telling him everything he wanted to know? Still, he was the pastor whom God had sent to them. Perhaps they could learn from an approach like this. It sounded more like something they would be doing in business than in their church. But they were glad to do as he asked.

Redwood Chapel had the usual complement of boards. There was the Board of Deacons, the Board of Missions, the Board of Christian Education, the Board of Trustees, and so on. Most churches have much the same organizational structure and for much the same reason. Nearly everybody does it that way.

Williams had some definite ideas about reorganizing that area of the church, but he said nothing about it right then. He wanted to get the men involved in his ideas of developing a total church ministry, and to let them see the value of such planning. There would be time enough to try to sell them on adopting a more effective organizational structure later.

He led the group of board chairmen into a discussion of the goals that should be evident in their church program. At first the answers came easily, off the top of their heads.

"We want to be a friendly church," one man said.

"A church of prayer."

"And worship."

"And evangelism."

It began to seem as though such a discussion was a waste of time, that everyone knew what the goals of the church should be. But the new pastor had expected such a response. Those were among the first goals most people suggested.

Important as they were, the group had to go further, stripping their ideas of fuzzy thinking and evangelical jargon, establishing concepts that were easy to understand.

For the next few Monday nights they studied the Book of Acts carefully in an effort to discover principles which the early Christians considered important. Those concepts were easy to find. The men listed the purposes of the church as they perceived them:

Doctrine

Prayer

Worship

Teaching

Witnessing

Fellowship

These were the elements, the leaders of Redwood Chapel decided, that should make up the philosophy of their church. They were the reason for the Chapel's existence.

"By this time the men were beginning to see where our approach could take us," Williams explains, "and were excited about it. They saw that those goals were the links in a chain that could bind them together and make them more effective than ever before."

In one sense the goals formed an endless chain. Witnessing would bring new converts. Through worship, prayer, fellowship, the teaching of doctrine and the Scriptures, the new believers would be brought to the place of spiritual and moral maturity. Then they would win others and the process would be repeated. The effectiveness of the church would be multiplied over and over.

Once the broad goals that made up the philosophy of the Chapel were established, the leaders were ready to move on to the evaluation phase of this new project. Critically they examined what was being done through their Sunday School, missions, the youth department, music, and every other avenue of service within the church.

"It is easy for a congregation like ours to get sidetracked by emphasizing one department above another," the new pastor told them. "If it were just a matter of making one area stronger than the others, it wouldn't be quite so critical. But what usually happens when we begin to work harder in one phase is that others are sadly neglected. It isn't long until the whole thrust of the ministry is thrown off balance."

When the evaluation had progressed far enough, they made a chart of the various departments of the church and the progress in them. It helped them see better what was happening in every area.

The men were astonished.

"If anyone had told me our ministry is so uneven and out of balance," one of them said, "I'd have said he didn't know what he was talking about."

"I thought we were doing about as well as we could expect to do in most departments," someone else put in. "I wonder how many years we'd have plugged along, satisfied that we've been doing our best for God, if it hadn't been for these Monday night meetings."

They began to consider which department of the church needed the most attention and decided it was the Sunday School. This important arm of the church was far from living up to its potential. In fact they soon saw that it was only limping along. It was soaking up a great deal of time and effort without really accomplishing much. The Sunday School was the first department they were going to have to overhaul.

The discussion of the Sunday School led them to other agencies within the church and the organizational framework under which they operated.

"Speaking of organization," one of the men exclaimed, "I wonder if we ought to take a long look at the hodgepodge of boards this committee represents. There has got to be a better way of running things. My business wouldn't last a year under such a cumbersome setup."

The Reorganization of Redwood Chapel

The church decided it would be more effective to have one board of 16 men. There should be a chairman and a church clerk to handle the general board meetings. The 14 remaining deacons would be paired off to head seven committees.

Originally, there were four "direct ministry" committees:
Worship
Teaching
Training
Extension
There were also three "supportive ministry" committees:
Social and Promotion
Property
Finance
While the first four were directly involved in carrying on the

teaching, training, worship, and outreach ministries of the church, the other three supported that work in the provision of property, funds, and publicity.

Later (in 1972) two more committees were added, one in each category, and the board expanded to 20 deacons (see chart, next page).

Membership and Visitation. This committee took over some of the duties of the Extension Committee: namely, those directly related to the immediate church family.

Sight and Sound Committee. An additional "supportive ministry" committee was established to develop and oversee the audiovisual areas which had originally been a responsibility of the Property Committee. This was made necessary by the increased TV and radio outreach.

"The people who head up these committees and are on our General Board are elected by the congregation after being presented to it by a nominating committee," Williams says. "In addition we have a special personnel committee which goes over the qualifications of the various members to evaluate their talents, training, and abilities. They develop a list of those they feel are qualified for each appointive position."

In 1963, two years after Williams' arrival, the church moved to a new location, building two Christian education units and a beautiful sanctuary seating 700. This was the first step in a master plan which now includes a new multipurpose building housing gynasium, adult class rooms, TV studios, and an office complex, and three additional Christian education units.

"What *Must* We Do?"

In 1966 after five years of solid growth the church took another long look at itself. The first meeting was a brainstorming session held after a Sunday evening service. No idea was too wild to be mentioned. The pastor asked those present to think

Organizational Chart for Redwood Chapel, 1974

```
                        CONGREGATION
                            |
                         PASTOR
                            |
                      CHURCH STAFF
                            |
                    NOMINATING COMMITTEE
```

CHAIRMAN	WORSHIP	TEACHING	TRAINING	MEMBERSHIP & VISITATION	CHURCH EXTENSION	SIGHT & SOUND	PROPERTY	SOCIAL & PROMOTION	FINANCE	SECRETARY
1	2	2	2	2	2	2	2	2	2	1 (Membership)

MINISTERING COMMITTEES

Chairman, Deacon Co-Ch., Deacon Deaconess *3 members at large	Chairman, Deacon Co-Ch. (SS Supt.) Deaconess *3 members at large	Chairman, Deacon Co-Ch., Deacon Deaconess *3 members at large	Chairman, Deacon Co-Ch., Deacon Deaconess *2 members at large **Board Sec. **Director of Spiritual Counselors	Chairman, Deacon Co-Ch., Deacon Deaconess *2 members at large **Men's Fellowship Pres. **Women's Miss. Fellowship President
Responsibilities	Responsibilities	Responsibilities	Responsibilities	Responsibilities
Pulpit Supply Children's Church Music Ushering Ordinances	Sunday School Vacation Bible School Released Time	Youth Program Training Hour Teacher Training Summer Camping	Visitation Membership Interviews Personnel File Benevolence Fund	Home and Foreign Missionary Outreach Evangelism

SUPPORTIVE COMMITTEES

Chairman, Deacon Co-Ch., Deacon Deaconess *3 members at large	Chairman, Deacon Co-Ch., Deacon *3 members at large	Chairman, Deacon Co-Ch., Deacon Deaconess *3 members at large	Chairman, Deacon (Treasurer) Co-Ch., Deacon (Finance Sec'y) Deaconess *3 members at large
Responsibilities	Responsibilities	Responsibilities	Responsibilities
Communication outreach Audio-Visual Equipment	Building Maintenance Equipment	Promotion Publicity Social Program (General)	Annual Budget Salary Review Handling Church monies Raising Finances

* Three members at large: One shall be responsible for the interests of children; one for youth; one for adult, with the exception of the Church Extension Committee which shall include two members at large—one for children, one for youth, plus the president of the Men's Fellowship and the Women's Missionary Fellowship.

** Ex-officio

about what they would like to see the church do if they had all the money needed for any project at home or anywhere in the world, and all the trained people necessary to carry it out successfully.

"We all have a tendency to limit our thinking when it comes to the Lord's work," Williams said. "Right now, I want us to break out of that straitjacket."

The discussion was lively and interesting, and it produced some startling ideas. When it had gone on for some time the question was changed slightly.

"What *could* we do?" Pastor Williams asked them.

The wilder schemes began to fall away. Obviously they couldn't give a Bible to every person in India or buy prime TV time on the three major networks for an hour-long Gospel program for 26 weeks a year.

They could, however, provide Bibles for one missionary to use in two or three villages in his country of service. They could have an occasional TV program on a local station.

And so it went.

The third question was even more specific.

"What *should* we do?"

Again the number of projects and programs dwindled. Those who spoke gave their reasons for feeling some particular program should be launched immediately. Not everyone agreed on every proposal by any means, and no church could have launched all of them in a given year. Though each was within the ability and resources of the Chapel, collectively they far exceeded anything one congregation of their size could hope to do in such a short period.

The last question further narrowed it down.

"What *must* we do?"

By now the questions were getting harder. What did God expect of them? What did He want them to do with the finances and staff they had? What was immaterial? What was vital and ought to be launched immediately?

At the next of the two annual retreats for the General Board each year, the projects most prominently mentioned in response to the last three questions were discussed. Prayerfully, priorities and goals were established.

"It's interesting to look back on that meeting," the pastor says now, "and see how many of the ideas that seemed so far out then have actually come into being. A TV ministry, a Christian day school, and branch churches were all suggested. Even I thought they were beyond any reasonable hope of reality. Today all three exist. I'm convinced we have them because God gave us the vision to think beyond ourselves and our limitations. He inspired us to establish goals and priorities and to get moving."

In 1961 the various board chairmen on the original committee the pastor had asked for worked long and hard on the goals and priorities that would guide them over the coming years. In the result, Pastor Williams' basic philosophy of what makes an effective congregation shows through.

He believes that as many people as possible have to be involved in the work of the church. Too many Christians in all congregations just come to services Sunday after Sunday, doing nothing more than occupying space. They make no significant contribution to the ministry of the church they profess to love, apart from the check they drop into the collection plate.

"They soak up what the minister has to say, but because they don't do anything for Jesus Christ," he explains, "they tend to sour. It isn't long until they are warped and bigoted, without the capacity to do much of anything worthwhile. I think the 'soak and sour' crowd represents the greatest single waste in the Christian church today."

He also has definite ideas about spreading the work around

the congregation so the major load will not fall on a few.

"The programming has to consider the fact that man does not exist for the church alone," he says. "I know of churches that will have something for their people every night of the week and quote the number who attend all the services as proof of their spiritual depth. I don't look at it that way."

Williams doesn't want the church to demand so much of people's time that they neglect their families.

"There has to be a balance in an individual's life, just as there must be a balance in the total program of an effective church," he says.

Total Church Program Day

Though it was not a part of the activities of Redwood Chapel the first few years, the first Saturday of September is now set aside as TCP (TOTAL CHURCH PROGRAM) DAY. It has become one of the most important all-church workers' events of the year.

It starts with a challenging guest speaker at breakfast at 8 A.M. and continues all day. The people divide into age-graded workshops. Sunday School teachers, Children's Church workers, boys and girls club leaders are all brought together according to the ages of the kids with whom they work.

"We feel this is very important," Pastor Williams says. "Sometimes we become so involved in our own sphere of activity that we don't see anything else. We lose sight of the fact that our ministry is a part of the whole. Getting everyone together to discuss methods and exchange ideas helps us realize that every activity contributes to the overall program."

Other workshops are set up according to the activity or ministry of the workers. Those primarily involved in music, for example, would be in one workshop.

There is a luncheon for the entire group at noon. The guest

speaker brings another message before the afternoon sessions, a continuation of the morning workshops, begin.

"We've always been concerned about unity and balance in our church activities," Sherman Williams explains, "The TOTAL CHURCH PROGRAM DAY helps to achieve it."

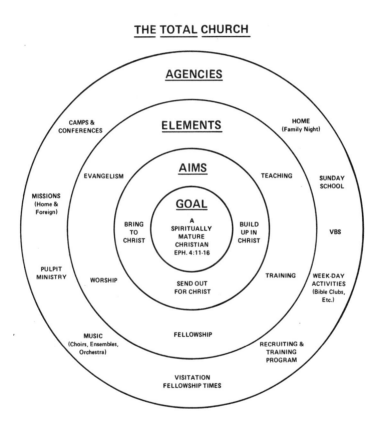

THE TOTAL CHURCH

AGENCIES

ELEMENTS

AIMS

GOAL

A SPIRITUALLY MATURE CHRISTIAN EPH. 4:11-16

BRING TO CHRIST

BUILD UP IN CHRIST

SEND OUT FOR CHRIST

EVANGELISM

TEACHING

WORSHIP

TRAINING

FELLOWSHIP

CAMPS & CONFERENCES

HOME (Family Night)

MISSIONS (Home & Foreign)

SUNDAY SCHOOL

VBS

PULPIT MINISTRY

WEEK-DAY ACTIVITIES (Bible Clubs, Etc.)

MUSIC (Choirs, Ensembles, Orchestra)

RECRUITING & TRAINING PROGRAM

VISITATION FELLOWSHIP TIMES

The total church philosophy foremost at Redwood Chapel, is clearly defined (see chart, page 39), and links every activity with the others.

"From Him [Christ] the whole body, joined and held together by every supporting ligament, grows and builds itself up in love, as each part does its work" (EPH. 4:16).

2

Sunday School on the Grow

In liberal circles the Sunday School has fallen on difficult days. Attendance is sagging and few consider it more than a nice place for children to be on Sunday morning. Yet in the thinking of most evangelicals, the Sunday School still forms the backbone of Christian education.

Sherman Williams had long considered the Sunday School to be the most important program of the local congregation. He had also discovered something in his years of traveling that increased his esteem for the Sunday School. Regardless of what else a local congregation did or did not do, it was often judged by its Sunday School, both by unbelievers and by those in the Christian community.

The Sunday School was considered a mirror that revealed the effectiveness, or lack of it, of the entire church program. If the Sunday School was vigorous and growing, the church would be looked on as having the same strength. For this reason and the fact that the committee's evaluation revealed glaring weaknesses in their Sunday School, Redwood Chapel decided to start with that department in attempting to make the church more effective.

"We not only wanted to increase our Sunday School's effectiveness as a tool for reaching our own church people and those in the community, but we wanted to build the reputation of our church," Williams recalls.

Even before the committee finished its work back in 1961, Pastor Williams was well aware of most of the reasons their Sunday School was not as vital as they thought it was. He had observed its operation briefly, and it fit only too well into a familiar pattern. In his travels around the country Williams had been appalled at the tragic waste of effort and opportunities caused by the poor quality of teaching in the average Sunday School.

However, he said nothing about it to anyone, except his wife. The people had to reach the place where they realized their errors themselves before they would be concerned enough to correct them. As a leader he would direct and guide and try to persuade, but he did not believe that being pastor of a church gave him the right to dictate its policies.

The leaders saw the problem, as he was sure they would, as soon as they gathered enough information to weigh the effectiveness of their Sunday School.

"Pastor," one of the men announced near the close of one meeting, "I've always been proud of the job our Sunday School has done. We've been careful to get sound material and have dedicated Christians teaching all the classes. I knew it wasn't as large as I'd like to have seen it, but I thought we were doing about as well as anyone could expect us to do. I guess I've been like an ostrich with my head in the sand. Will you help us train our teachers so we can do the kind of a job we have always thought we were doing?"

Would he? That was exactly what he had been waiting and praying for. By training the Sunday School teachers he could multiply his own effectiveness many times. As far as he was concerned, this was the place to start to get the church off dead center and moving forward.

Teacher Training

Pastor Williams had already been working on a plan for training the teachers, anticipating the concern of the board as they saw the true situation. Now that they were recommending it, he selected a course of study and found a time that was suitable for most of the teachers. They began to meet from 6 to 6:45 P.M. on Sundays, just prior to the evening services.

There were other changes he wanted to make in the Sunday School as well. The records were not as complete as he would have liked to see them, and they needed a simple way of monitoring a teacher's follow-up calls to see that they were being made regularly. He also wanted to inaugurate a recruiting system for bringing those with teaching ability into training classes so they could get new people involved in teaching. If his plans for the Sunday School were adopted they would need far more teachers than they had at present. There were many ways he felt the Sunday School could be improved, but training the teachers was the most important. There would be time for the other changes later.

The Sunday School made progress with the inauguration of the teacher-training sessions, but the pastor was not entirely satisfied. Something more was needed—a spurt of interest or activity that would focus attention on their Sunday School— something that would get people excited about it. Then the 1967 Sunday School Contest, sponsored by the National Sunday School Association, was announced. Williams had never been one for contests, but this one intrigued him.

"It's coming at exactly the right time," he told his wife. "I believe our entering it would challenge our people in a way that would really help our Sunday School."

He had correctly read the situation and the mood of the people. They needed the impetus entering the contest would give and vigorously threw themselves into it. Competing with churches of many denominations all across the country, Redwood Chapel not only won in its size category but won the grand prize for greatest growth.

More important, their Sunday School was on the move. The drive sparked by the contest continued, pushing enrollment and attendance upward, even as the training program improved the quality of the teaching. Thus, the church was awakened to the importance of the Sunday School.

But Pastor Williams had other concerns. He knew that Christians can grow cold, spiritually, if they aren't ministered to. He had found it a problem himself.

"I know how difficult it is for me when I have to preach every Sunday without the opportunity of hearing the Word preached by someone else," he explains. "I've been concerned about our Sunday School teachers for the same reason. Most of them are in the preaching services, but they need to be taught in Sunday School part of the time, as well."

Since teacher-training classes had provided a sufficient number of trained substitutes another step forward could be taken. Teachers could be rotated, giving the regular teaching staff a rest and allowing substitutes to gain on-the-job experience.

The regular staff takes the teaching responsibilities for one quarter. The second quarter they trade places with their substitutes. That way all have an opportunity to sit under other teachers and receive their ministry.

"We aren't the only church to use that system," Williams says, "but there aren't many who do it."

Additional Staff

In 1971, when the need for a minister of Christian education at Redwood Chapel became apparent, Williams thought of one man, his brother-in-law Winston Miller. He was also serving the Lord in publishing, having been a Christian education consultant/salesman for 15 years. He was somewhat older than the average Christian ed director. Most churches looked for a young man, thinking he would be more apt to have new ideas and be able to relate better to the youth. Williams was looking for an additional set of qualities, however. He wanted someone who shared his own views regarding the methods needed to have an effective church with an aggressive Christian Education Department.

Miller was such a man. In addition he had the background of knowledge from working at Sunday School conventions to implement the changes. By any standard the senior pastor applied, his brother-in-law was the best choice.

When Miller came to Redwood Chapel, one of his first tasks was to work out a series of guidebooks for the workers of his department. He had seen the value of such booklets in many churches that had tried them.

"You have to let a person know what is expected of him before either of you can tell whether he's doing a good piece of work or not," he says. "In fact, in many cases the guidebook can be a big factor in the success of a dedicated teacher, Sunday School secretary, or superintendent."

Teacher Standards and Recruitment

Miller planned to devise guidelines for the workers in every activity under his care, and eventually did. Like Pastor Williams, however, he started with the Sunday School. He developed job descriptions for teachers, departmental superintendents, and secretaries, explaining in detail just what their duties were. He told the teachers when they were expected to be at the church on Sunday morning, what was to be done before the kids came, how to handle discipline, and how to make follow-up calls on absentees.

"We leave as little unexplained as possible," he says.

He also worked out a covenant the teachers are asked to sign yearly. The teacher agrees to live before his pupils in such a way that he will be an example to them and to discharge the duties of his office faithfully.

"It's been very helpful," Miller says. "People have a tendency to place the same importance on a position that those delegating the authority place on it. When they see that we consider the job of teaching important enough to ask them to make a covenant with the Lord and the church regarding it, they have a deeper concern for what they are doing. I believe it shows them the value of being a Sunday School teacher and gives them added incentive in their responsibilities."

Teachers are appointed for a period of one year and must be reappointed to continue to serve. Individual teacher records are kept, showing what services they have attended, the follow-up calls that have been assigned to them, and what they did with them. The superintendents and the staff know how effectively the teachers conduct their classes, whether they have attended the monthly worker's conference, if they have taken the training course, and how well they attended the classes. All of these things go into a teacher's record and are a guide to reappointment.

"The fact that they are appointed for only one year at a time makes it easier to change teachers if we feel it is necessary," Miller explains. "When we decide an individual isn't as effective with his class as he ought to be, we try to transfer him to some other program. So far, that has worked out quite well."

Recruiting new teachers for the Sunday School at Redwood Chapel is as much of a problem as it is anywhere else. Periodically a talent survey is made of the entire congregation to determine the area in which a person is willing, and best qualified, to serve. Questions are asked about special interests, abilities, and training that could be of value in the church program. The survey keeps Miller and the rest of the staff abreast of the talent available and any changes in personal situations that may make it possible for an individual to assume a new responsibility in the Sunday School or church.

"A mother with small children is a good example," Miller says. "She may have felt too burdened to take a class when the kids were toddlers, but as they get older she may not be tied down so tightly. Then there are people who have excellent training and background for teaching a Sunday School class but are too shy to approach anyone. Our talent survey uncovers those people and makes them visible and available to us."

The church also learns the abilities and interests of those who enroll in the Membership Orientation Class. At the beginning of the final session, each one is given a PRIVILEGE AND RESPONSIBILITY QUESTIONNAIRE. This three-page form lists all the jobs in the Sunday School, in other agencies of the Christian Education Department, and in the entire church. It is designed to find out what special skills, experience, and interests each new member has and the areas in which he is willing to serve.

The form is filled out and handed to the pastor at the close of the class period. The information is transferred to a computer, along with the facts that come in from the Talent

Survey, providing a "bank" of information about members—their gifts, potential, and abilities.

"When we start looking for new teachers," the Minister of Christian Education explains, "we go to the computer 'bank' first for qualified prospects. It's amazing how many excellent workers are uncovered simply by asking what our people have done, what they can do, and what they would like to do. It's as simple as that."

The personnel committee goes over the qualifications of every teacher (and every other worker in the church, as well). If nobody on the committee knows the person, someone goes out and interviews him before he is approached about assuming any responsibility. In some cases those who aren't members are given a temporary assignment but only members are given permanent posts.

A salesman in the congregation has worked out a Recruitment Chart for enlisting the services of individuals the church can use. The chart gives a quick look at the various jobs, such as Sunday School teacher, Children's Church worker, and youth sponsor.

"We try to get a backlog of workers, so we are continually recruiting, trying to get people lined up to fill vacancies as they occur."

Sunday School Records

The records kept on pupils in the Sunday School are as complete as those on the teaching staff.

"Ours is a fairly large Sunday School," Miller says. "I think we're all conscious of that fact, and the dangers of being large. It's quite possible than an individual, or an entire family, can be 'lost' in a group the size of ours.

"If the records aren't adequate, people can become careless in attendance and even quit coming altogether without anyone on the staff being aware of it. For this reason we have worked out a set of individual attendance forms that provide us with all the information we need to keep up with our people."

Many churches use visitors' cards. Most have permanent Sunday School records that note attendance and absence. At Redwood Chapel, however, far more information is recorded. The teacher is asked to note any personal discipline problems in addition to any special characteristics, needs, and progress. This information can be invaluable.

One Sunday a lad in the Junior Department was such a discipline problem his teacher was close to tears. "He won't pay attention to anything I say and causes so much trouble he disrupts the entire class," she told her superintendent.

At the moment she was certain the boy was acting out of meanness and should be forced to shape up or be sent home. A look at his card, however, revealed that his mother had died suddenly two months before. His father, unable to keep him at home and work, had placed him with foster parents. In addition to the boy's grief, he was torn by feelings of rejection and not being wanted. His trouble-making, far from expressing deliberate belligerence, was in reality a desperate, lonely cry for love and help.

She had to discipline him. There were others in the class to think of and he could not be allowed to ruin the effectiveness of the class for them. Still, there was a difference now that she knew the reason for his actions. Her punishment was tempered with understanding and love. He soon learned that she did love him and was concerned about him. He stopped disrupting the class and before the end of the year had made a decision for Christ and was a model pupil. Proper records helped make it possible for the teacher to understand and help him.

Attendance is also given close attention, and absentees are

carefully followed up. The Sunday School secretary assigns up to four absentees and/or visitors to each teacher for follow-up each week. He is given a sheet with names, addresses, and phone numbers of those with whom he is to get in touch. After he calls he notes the results on the sheet, which he returns to the secretary. He notes that the pupil was ill, away from home for the Sunday, or is losing interest. In many cases the show of concern on the part of the teacher is enough to get the pupil back.

One 13-year-old girl stopped coming to Sunday School for several weeks. When her teacher phoned she was candid. "I went to visit my grandma for awhile and when I got back I was in the habit of sleeping late on Sunday morning."

The following Sunday was no different from the others, so far as she was concerned. She missed several times in a row, but her teacher did not write her off. She continued to call, letting her know she was missed and that everyone would like to have her back. It wasn't long until she had returned to her class and was once more under the influence of the Gospel.

She learned that somebody cared.

"With each teacher making four follow-up calls each week, if they have that many absentees," Miller continues, "we are in touch with a large number of people each week. We have 80 Sunday School classes. That would give us a possible 320 follow-up calls by telephone or personal visit. This sort of close contact shows the kids that we really love them. It helps keep our attendance up and ties us closer to the families our teachers have visited."

The information on the attendance cards is available to other Sunday School teachers, the workers in other departments of the church, and the staff. For example, those involved in Children's Church often go to the Sunday School files to find out about certain children. This sort of information makes it possible for them to help some of the pupils with counseling and guidance they could not have been given otherwise. You have to know a problem exists before you can make an intelligent effort to solve it.

Contrary to one present trend in education promoted by some secular authorities, Redwood Chapel uses graded report cards for the children in the younger departments. These have been helpful in securing better pupil attention, more faithful attendance, and punctuality.

"We've found that the kids from preschoolers through the Junior departments look forward to getting their report cards. There's a sense of accomplishment that is important to them. That's especially true if they get a grade of 90 or above. We call those our 'honor students' and put a gold seal on their report cards for the quarter."

They also grade the teachers and select the "teacher of the quarter" for each department on the basis of the grading. "We're planning to give a 'teacher of the year' award for the teacher in our entire Sunday School who has the best grade," Miller continues. "It's part of our continuing program to stress quality for our teaching staff."

Innovations for Adults

After checking the adult Sunday School records and visiting some of the adult classes, Miller came to realize that *some* new converts were having trouble surviving in the adult Sunday School classes. Most of the adult teachers were gearing their lessons to the long-time Christians, and teaching over the heads of the new converts. These people simply did not have the Bible background to understand what was going on.

To remedy this, Miller decided to start a special class for new converts and non-Christian adults. As teacher, he chose a businessman in the church who had been a Christian only a year himself. However, he had become a real student of the Bible and was enthusiastically involved in several Christian activities. He had not been involved in church activities long enough to pick up the theological "jargon" that many adult teachers use.

In discussing the need of such a class with the prospective teacher, Miller discovered that the man himself had found it difficult to understand what had been taking place in the adult classes. "It took me about six months to figure out what they were talking about," he said.

Pastor Miller gave him a number of resource materials to study. This study was to cover basic doctrine, apologetics, how to apply the Bible to life, the meaning of Bible terms, and the mechanics of Bible usage. All of this was to be taught in lay-man's terms. Theological terms were banned unless they were being studied to discover their meaning. The course was designed so a person could enter at any time, continue for six months, and graduate when the study reached the point where he had entered. Many non-Christians who began with the class have been won to faith in Christ through its ministry.

Another innovation in Redwood Chapel's Adult Sunday School is their Circle Classes. "I used to walk across our big gym floor on Sunday mornings and it bothered me," Miller says. "Here we had all of this space and we were not putting it to good use."

In cooperation with the Social and Promotion Committee, round tables six feet in diameter were purchased. Ten people can sit comfortably at each table. Six adult classes were grouped together to comprise two Circle groups. There are 12 table classes in Circle I, meeting at the 9:30 hour, and 8 in Circle II, at 11 o'clock.

During each Circle session, eight people are assigned to each table, with one person designated as the discussion leader. It is the responsibility of the eight people at each table to invite visitors and fill the two vacant chairs each Sunday, making a table group of 10.

A Master Teacher was chosen for each of the two sessions. He trains the discussion leaders for his circle in a training session each Sunday morning from 9:00 to 9:30. He lays the groundwork at that time for the discussion groups during the class period. The programs at 9:30 and at 11 follow this pattern:

Open assembly—10 minutes

    This is used to promote class activities, sharing, prayer requests, and prayer

Lesson from the Master Teacher—30 minutes

Discussion time at the tables—30 minutes

"The classes have been in operation only four months and already impressive gains have been made in attendance, with total attendance running from 20% to 30% over one year ago," Miller says. He expects to grow to 300 in each session.

Each table group is also a fellowship unit. They are to shepherd one another from week to week, with the discussion leader having the over-all supervision of follow-up. Each table group has a get-together in one of their homes periodically with several table groups getting together for an occasional larger social event. In a larger church, this draws the people who would normally stay on the periphery into the class activities. It also allows the adult to share his experiences from the Word or personal life with the other members of his table group in an informal setting. "It is surprising how active each one becomes in the small circle of his table group," reports Miller.

Handling Expansion

Redwood Chapel Sunday School saw a gain in attendance over

the years until facilities bulged with 900 people, and there was no more room for additional classes.

"We knew we couldn't build a new educational unit at the time," Pastor Williams explains. "Costs were in the stratosphere and climbing every month—much faster than our ability to pay them. Besides, it didn't seem practical to build more facilities that would be used just an hour or two each week."

So the board decided on double sessions for the Sunday School, at 9:30 and 11 A.M. Others in California and elsewhere had done it successfully, but the staff and board at Redwood Chapel approached the innovation with certain reservations.

"We had made a lot of changes in our Sunday School in the past few years," Miller says, "but this was the most far-reaching thing we had tried. It involved altering drastically the habits of our people, and that is always a serious matter. We did a lot of praying that the Double Session Sunday School would be accepted."

The decision did not create two complete Sunday Schools, which would have called for a duplication of the program and might have ended with one still overcrowded and the other small and ineffective. Rather, the division was made according to age-levels. Those up to a certain age had Sunday School the first hour and Children's Church the second. The other group had Children's Church first and then went to Sunday School.

The following chart shows how the double session Sunday School at Redwood Chapel is arranged:

9:30	11:00
2-year-olds Sunday School	2-year-olds Church
3-year-olds Sunday School	3-year-olds Church

4-year-olds Sunday School
5-year-olds Sunday School
1st grade Church
2nd grade Sunday School
3rd grade Church
4th grade Sunday School
5th grade Sunday School
6th grade Church
High School Sunday School

4-year-olds Church
5-year-olds Church
1st grade Sunday School
2nd grade Church
3rd grade Sunday School
4th grade Church
5th grade Church
6th grade Sunday School
Junior High Sunday School

Adult Department

All ages—Circle I (includes former Berean, Crusader, Disciples, and King's classes)
18-25 young marrieds "Carpenters"
36-40 "Sojourners"
All ages—new converts "Know and Grow"

Adult Department

All ages—Circle I (includes former Builders and Fabulous Forties classes)
18-20 college freshmen and sophomores—"Kappa Chi"
21-25 college upperclassmen "Maranatha"
26-45 women "Sowers"
46 and up women "Evangels"
36 and up men "Fishers of Men"

"We publicized the change for three months in advance of January 1973, the target date for launching the new program," Miller continues. "We anticipated a certain amount of difficulty but were surprised at how well it went off. The change was made with a minimum of confusion and grumbling. In a couple of Sundays everything was going smoothly. I don't think anyone would want to turn the clock back to a single-session Sunday School now.

"Actually," he says, "our new approach has given us greater stability in attendance and has even caused our attendance and enrollment to increase in some departments. There are families on the fringe who had their kids in Sunday School but those kids had never gone to Children's Church until we made the change. Now they are sort of forced to participate in that phase of our program, too. They have kids in both sections of the Sunday School and want to make one trip to get the family there and back. So our solution to the Sunday School problem has strengthened our TOTAL CHURCH PROGRAM."

"Therefore go and make disciples . . . teaching them to obey everything I have commanded you" (MATT. 28:19-20).

3

Christian Education Beyond Sunday School

Mention Christian education and most church members think only of the Sunday School. There is another side of the coin, however. In their desire to develop a TOTAL CHURCH PROGRAM, the staff and board at Redwood Chapel have given careful attention to all the related activities that should be a part of the ministry of an alert, aggressive church. There are the Children's Church, the Wednesday night Kids Clubs for the younger age groups, and girls and boys clubs for juniors and early teens.

Children at Worship

Children's Church is an important phase of the Christian ed program. It is a worship service geared to the interests and level of understanding of the children involved. The graded program begins with the two-year-olds and goes up to include the sixth-graders, with 11 groups meeting in all. It is as thoroughly planned and as carefully executed as the Sunday School.

Leaders use messages, stories, and films to present Jesus Christ in words and illustrations the children can understand. Quite naturally, evangelism is one of the most important elements of the program.

"And it works," says a grateful father, who is also much involved in Children's Church. "We had heard from members of the staff and other workers that they had kids receive Christ because of Children's Church. You can't imagine how thrilled we were when our own daughter made her decision to receive Him two years ago in one of our meetings. She was eight years old at the time. I can tell you, it was like a benediction on our ministry in this department. It seemed as though God was showing us in a very special way the worth of what we were doing."

A woman staff member mentions the advantage of freeing parents to work in other departments of the church or to allow them to give full attention to the worship service. "We don't like to think of ourselves as a baby-sitting service," she explains, "but in one way we do serve that function."

Though the wide range of ages involved in Children's Church makes it impossible to use the same program throughout, there is a basic philosophy that guides the entire department.

"We start with the premise that the kids will not be interested in the adult service," Bob Jensen, who heads up the program for the older group, says. "And we didn't want to give them a variation of their Sunday School class. They had just come from that."

The program would have to be varied to hold the interest of their young members. It would have to have a strong Bible emphasis and a worship service at the children's levels of understanding.

"We are actually preparing them to move into the adult service," one of the department workers says. "For this reason the services need to be somewhat formal and related to the worship services of the older age groups so the kids will be prepared for moving up when promotion time comes."

They also train them for leadership by getting as many as possible to participate.

"It's important to get them used to being in front of a group of people while they're young. We get them to read the Scriptures, lead the singing, have special music, lead in prayer, and take the offering."

The kids themselves attest to the value of a program geared directly to them.

"You ought to come to *our* church," a mischievous dark-eyed lad of five exclaimed. "It's really neat, Mom."

The sense of ownership by the kids is carefully cultivated. They aren't bored as they so often are when they are forced to sit through an adult service they cannot understand. They are constantly being challenged, and they respond with such wholeheartedness that it causes them to look forward eagerly to each promotion day, when they advance to another level of Children's Church.

The program for the sixth-graders is divided into three segments, and the members are divided into three groups. Each group takes its turn in handling the preliminaries. One of their number reads the Scripture, someone else leads the singing, another takes up the offering, and someone has the morning prayer. Several minutes are devoted to getting prayer requests from the children.

The second segment is lighter, giving the kids a chance to get rid of some of their exuberance so they can settle down for the worship portion of the program. They sing choruses, have Bible drills, quizzes, and contests.

One month they studied the Book of John. They were assigned five chapters to read each week. All the quizzes, drills, and contests were based on those chapters.

"We have used some prepared material," Jensen said, "but most of the time we work up our own questions."

The third and final segment of the program is devoted to a worship service. This is similar to the adult service, but shorter. Thus, in another year, when the sixth-graders go into the regular church service, they will be prepared for it. The children themselves are used for as much of the service as possible. An adult usually leads the brief song service, and another brings the message. When the leaders have chosen a major theme, it often will be used for as long as six weeks, and the same person will speak each week.

"We do that so the theme will be developed logically and with some semblance of order," one of the workers says. "We're careful to choose speakers who can relate to a young audience. They've got to be able to present the Gospel in a simple way without talking down to the children. And they've got to be interesting, to hold the attention of that gang out front. It isn't the easiest thing to do."

When the kids are finally promoted to the adult service, the feelings of responsibility and ownership are still with them. The other programs have been uniquely theirs. Now that they are big enough and old enough to go to the regular adult service with their parents, they feel it belongs to them too. This is what Miller and his workers in the Children's Church have been striving for.

"We see a definite and progressive spiritual growth in the kids," one of the staff says. "I'm convinced Children's Church is a strong link in the chain that pulls them toward Christian maturity. I'm positive, as well, that it helps us to cut down on the dropouts that seem to plague every church as their teenagers approach adulthood."

Club Programs

The girls and boys club programs fill an important place in the lives of the kids they serve and are given special attention at Redwood Chapel. However, the planning group was concerned about those who were too young to take part in the activities of those organizations. They were prompted by the TOTAL CHURCH PROGRAM concept, which pointed up a number of gaps in their ministry. This was one of them.

"So we worked out a program of our own for those from kindergarten through the second grade and called it Kids Club," Mrs. Helen Lee, who heads the project, explains.

The format differs from that of their Sunday School lessons or Children's Church. They didn't want it to be a replay of either program. Yet, it doesn't differ quite as much as it would if the kids were a bit older. Each week they are given a memory verse to learn. The following Wednesday night, when they come to the meeting, they are checked in and are given an opportunity to repeat it.

"It's surprising how hard they will work on those memory verses," Mrs. Lee says. "It is one of the items we check to see if they have earned a seal for the week."

They are asked if they have prayed before every meal all week and whether they came to the meeting on time. If they qualify in all three areas they are given a seal. It's only a little thing but the leaders attach importance to it and build it up in the eyes of the kids. It's a big thing to them.

In addition to the person who checks them in, someone is there to start a simple game that will keep the early ones busy until it is time for the meeting to start. Then they have a few minutes of singing, emphasizing action songs, which the kids love. Following that is a period of prayer.

"It has been amazing how eagerly the kids look forward to praying," Mrs. Lee says. "We try to add our efforts to others directed at teaching them to pray. We give them some items to praise God for and ask them to mention others of their own. When they have finished praising Him, we go to the requests, following the same pattern."

The kids do all the praying.

Then they divide into two groups and have their story. At times the workers will use a missionary account, told with flash cards or Suede-graph. On other occasions they will use a continued story, always concluding at some high point of interest. Wanting to find out what happened in the next installment makes the kids anxious to come back the following week. In many cases the parents aren't concerned about spiritual things and the kids have to provide the impetus to get there on Wednesday nights. The stories are chosen carefully and in consultation with the others who work with the same age-group so there will be no duplication.

After the story time they have a cookie and chocolate milk or a light refreshment. They review their memory verses once more and then conclude the evening's activities with handcraft or games.

"We're trying to get the children to put Bible principles into active use in their lives," one worker says. "We want them to begin building Christian character. We try to teach them to pray, to love the Word of God, and to have a strong interest in missions."

It isn't the type of program, with this age-group, where a great deal can be seen in the way of results. It is a time of seed-sowing, of beginning to develop attitudes and Christian integrity. For workers who see no visible results it can be, and often is, discouraging. It is quite easy to feel that nothing of lasting merit ever happens.

Still, there was the little fellow not long ago who stammered out his problem when an alert leader saw that he was morose and not entering into the activities with the other kids that evening. For him, his immediate difficulty was a weighty one. She was able to help him by pointing him to what the Bible says and explaining how it answers the situation that troubled him.

"He'll probably forget the reason for talking to me in a few weeks, if he hasn't forgotten it already," she explains. "Yet I like to think the lesson is one that could help him all his life. I tried to make him understand that Jesus Christ is the answer to all his difficulties, whatever they are."

She paused for a moment before going on, her eyes shining. "Somehow, being able to help him, even a little, makes it all worthwhile."

The majority of those who come to Wednesday night Kids Club are from within the church family, but at least a third are from unchurched homes. Among the latter group are children who first got interested because friends brought them. The Wednesday night meeting is one of the "hooks" that has brought boys and girls, and even entire families, into other areas of the church program. They may start with Kids Club but soon are interested in Sunday School or Children's Church or in getting their parents or an older brother or sister involved in some activity of Redwood Chapel.

"The program is definitely one of outreach," Mrs. Lee says. "That is one of the advantages of a wide-ranging church program such as ours, which has something for everyone. Get one member of a family involved in one phase of our ministry and there is a natural attraction for the others. This has been a means of winning many for Jesus Christ."

Two youth organizations take up where Kids Club leaves off and carry girls and boys well into their adolescent years. These are Christian Service Brigade and Pioneer Girls, each operated along the guidelines set down by their national organizations. In that, they are little different from many other such local groups elsewhere in the country. What makes them unique is their size and effectiveness and the part they play in the program of the church.

"We have an average of 90 girls and leaders in our girls' group," Winston Miller says. "And we have more than 100 boys in their group. A third of the boys and about the same percentage of the girls are from outside the church."

These activities provide two more avenues for the Chapel to use in reaching unbelievers in the community. For example, the boys club reached a boy we'll call Dick. Dick had some problems not shared by most boys his age. His IQ was lower than average and his attention span was short. All of his brief life he had been a failure at everything he tried, especially at school. He was no good at sports, had a lot of trouble with his grades, and wasn't particularly well liked by either his fellow students or his teachers.

"One of the good things that has come Dick's way has been our boys work," a boys club leader says. "From the first time he came it has been an important part of his life. He won't miss a Wednesday night."

A few months before our interview, Dick had put his trust in Christ for salvation. Since then a change had come over him. He had actually completed the second of eight ranks, even managing Bible memorization, which was difficult for him.

"It's amazing to see the change that's come over Dick in three short months."

Dads are invited regularly to the Wednesday night meetings, in addition to a number of events that particularly involve them. One father got involved in club work by helping with a camping trip his son was taking. He loved the outdoors himself, and soon got very interested in activities in that area. He did not confine his interest to camping and hiking, however, but began helping in other areas as well.

"It's been interesting to watch him," one of the men says. "He got more and more involved in the club, and at the same time he and his entire family began to attend other phases of our church program. None of them are believers yet, but we are praying that they will receive Christ."

Another man, a nominal Christian, claimed to be too busy to do anything except attend the worship services occasionally. Then his son became active in the boys club and, reluctantly, the father was drawn into the program. It wasn't long before he was more active in other phases of the church program and began to grow spiritually.

One Jewish family is currently being reached for Jesus Christ because they, too, have a son who became interested in the boys club. The boy's first contact with the Chapel was when he started attending club meetings. Not long after that he began to come to Sunday School. For a couple of years he was the only member of the family to attend anything at Redwood Chapel. Finally, he became a Christian.

Shortly after that kids and adults in the church began to invite his brother and sisters to other activities they thought would interest them. Recently his brother and one of his sisters received Christ.

One lad of nine got both of his parents interested in the Gospel. A friend had brought him to one of the club meetings.

"This is for me!" he exclaimed on the way home that Wednesday night. "It's great!"

From that time on he was one of the most eager guys in

the club. He soon became interested in the Word of God, and, on a camping trip some months later, he received Christ as his Saviour.

But the story didn't end there. He went back home and told his parents what had happened to him. They were in their early 40s and had some church background, so they understood something of what he was trying to tell them. That, however, wasn't what hit them the hardest. They were jarred out of their complacency and attracted to Christ by the change that had taken place in their son's life.

Because of what they were seeing in their son, they began to attend the morning services with him. Then they started coming on Sunday nights. At one of the Sunday evening services when Pastor Williams concluded a message on salvation and gave an invitation, they came forward. They took the same stand their son had a few months before.

"Actually," Winston Miller explains, "it was the boy who led them to Christ. They went forward at a church meeting but his testimony at home as he lived Christ was the deciding factor. They're in our Membership Orientation Class right now and will be baptized and taken into membership in a few weeks."

The leaders of the girls club have also seen the heart-warming results of their ministry.

"The spiritual growth of our girls is continuous," a leader says. "We can see it from month to month and we get glimpses of it in hearing their casual conversations with each other. That's when they reveal real changes in attitudes and convictions."

"That's right," another says. "When they get to talking about their problems at school and at home, we can begin to see that some of the principles of Christian living we keep stressing are getting through to them."

Another girls leader tells of having one of her girls come to her recently.

"She was under conviction as the result of the meeting and wanted to receive Christ."

They sat down together and went through a little booklet on salvation. When her guide was sure she understood exactly what was involved, she prayed with her.

"Yes," another worker with the girls club says, "we have girls who make decisions to receive Christ. It seems that it usually happens when we're out on an overnight trip or a hike—or some other time when we have an opportunity to spend time with the girls alone. The last girl I can recall came to me after a Bible study on an outing and wanted to know more about the Lord. She had been under conviction for several weeks, but it wasn't until we were away from all the activities of their busy little world that she thought seriously enough to reach a decision concerning Jesus Christ and her personal relationship with Him."

Both the boys and the girls clubs devote a portion of their time to helping others. The girls have a strong missionary interest and each of their groups chooses a mission project for the year. They also go to convalescent hospitals and make tray favors and small gifts for the people confined there.

Both boys and girls go to Harbor House, a joint church project for the underprivileged in Oakland, and help in any way they can. They have done painting there in addition to spending time with the kids who live in the neighborhood and frequent the House.

"We try to help our kids see that the work at Harbor House is only one phase of an entire area of concern in which we, as believers, should be interested. We want them to see that we have a definite responsibility to those who are less fortunate than we," Miller explained. "It's had a good effect on our youngsters and I like to think they have been helpful to some of the kids in the inner city."

Summer VBS Outreach

Vacation Bible School is always a big event at Redwood Chapel Community Church. In 1974 they had an enrollment of over 900 children with a high attendance of 777 and an average of 735. It is basically an outreach effort with a large percentage of the kids coming from unchurched homes in the area.

Their VBS philosophy is wrapped in evangelism. While Christian kids attend and there is a certain amount of Bible teaching, the main thrust is presenting Jesus Christ to those who don't know Him. The entire program is aimed in that direction.

The staff of 130, including secretaries and helpers, operates three separate divisions, each under a different director at a different location. The preschoolers through grade four use the regular Sunday School facilities. Grades five and six are in the gym. Grades seven and eight meet at the church but are bussed to a place where they have access to a large private swimming pool.

The cost of the Vacation Bible School program as Redwood Chapel conducts it is high—over $2,400 in 1974, even though volunteers plan and prepare the handwork so there is little cost for that. Interestingly, a letter from the committee to members of the congregation suggesting that they might wish to sponsor one or more children at $3 each brought in over half the amount needed to meet expenses in 1973 and 1974. The boys and girls brought a missionary offering during VBS which totalled $750.

"We don't make payment a condition for enrolling," one of the volunteer workers says, "but we have learned from experience that the kids whose parents have paid are more faithful in attendance than the others."

Evaluation sheets are passed out to the workers at the close of the last day asking for constructive criticism of the program and suggestions for improving it the following year. The form asks for an evaluation of each segment of the day's activities, individually. It also inquires how effective were the materials used, the missionary story, the music, contests, handcraft, and the closing rally. At the bottom workers are asked to list the names of those who are gifted in any areas that would be of help in the following year's program. Information from the forms is carefully analyzed.

"Those forms have been helpful in sharpening our programs," a staff member says. "And we often get the names of people who are terrific at counseling children or telling stories or helping with handcraft or some other skill badly needed in Bible School. We go over these evaluations right away, even before our committee has its first meeting in January to begin work on next year's Bible School."

There are always a large number of decisions for Christ at VBS, but follow up is frequently difficult. The summer months are times of vacations and many of the kids are away when the church visitors attempt to see them. It is often fall before contact is made, which lessens the effectiveness of the visits to some extent.

"I doubt that we have a program anywhere in the church that requires more time and effort than Vacation Bible School," Winston Miller says, "or is more rewarding."

The Day School

Redwood Christian School, a brainchild of the leadership of the church, uses the church's facilities during the week throughout the school year. It was organized in 1969, and in its fifth year had over 500 enrolled from kindergarten through tenth grade.

Though the school is set up as a separate corporation, its relationship to the church is very close. A number of the school board members are members of the church and the doctrine and philosophy that guide the school are compatible with those of the church.

"We have different gifts, according to the grace given us. If a man's gift is prophesying, let him use it in proportion to his faith. If it is serving, let him serve; if it is teaching, let him teach" (ROM. 12:6-7).

4

The Truth for Youth

"Don Larmour, our Minister of Youth, has been very good for Redwood Chapel in the more than two years he's been with us," Associate Pastor Neal Doty says. "His ministry is basically that of Bible teaching. When I was Redwood's Youth Minister, I tended to be pretty flamboyant. It takes a guy like Don to build solid, stable Christian lives." Larmour does his "building" in some 300 young lives, more than most pastors have in their entire congregations. The high school group averages 110 to 125 or so. The junior high and college-career groups are somewhat smaller, making the total of the three groups about 300.

The emphasis of the regular youth program is on Bible study, discipleship, and Christian leadership. In addition to the Sunday School classes which most of the youth attend, there are Bible studies for the high school and college groups on Wednesday night. Add all other programs and these young people could be involved in Bible study or training classes three times a week in addition to Sunday School and the Sunday worship services. Then there are special seminars that deal with specific problems such as dating and marriage.

"We try to help the kids relate Jesus Christ to every area of their lives," Larmour explains. "I know that's a paraphrase of Pioneer Girls' slogan, but it's the guideline we try to work with. Christianity is the most practical way of life anyone has ever discovered. We want our kids to know this."

At this writing the high schoolers were studying the life of Christ on Wednesday nights.

"It's quite a simple study," the youth pastor said. "We get right to the point. I do a certain amount of explaining but try to keep that to a minimum. Most of the time is devoted to asking questions and getting the kids to answer. What I'm striving for is to get them to do their own studying. The more involved in the Word we can get them, the faster they will grow spiritually and the more effective they will be in sharing their faith with others."

The Goals of Youth Work

Larmour has three goals in working with senior high school students. "In fact I'm convinced they should be the goals of every youth group," he says.

1. *The youth program should help the kids meet their spiritual needs.* That may be salvation, as it is in the case of those who have never made a personal commitment of their lives to Jesus Christ. It may be conquering pride or materialism or greed. It may be an unsaved boyfriend or girlfriend God wants the Christian young person to give up. It may be putting aside the sins of the world, or overcoming an unwillingness to allow Him to have full control of their lives.

"Whatever those needs are," the youth pastor says, "they have to be met before a person can be usable for God."

2. *The youth program should develop leadership.* Youthful Christians have to learn to use the skills and talents God has given them. The boy or girl who sits in the back row may have tremendous latent ability if it can be discovered and developed. By encouraging the kids to run as much of their own program as possible, Larmour hopes to find potential leaders and at the same time begin to develop the confidence and self-assurance they need to be used more effectively for Christ.

"I've seen leadership crop up in the most unexpected places," he explains. "Kids no one ever dreamed could do anything have blossomed after being guided through some responsibility. They have discovered they could actually do things as well as anyone else."

3. *The youth program should lead kids into a life of commitment and witnessing.* It isn't enough to bring unbelievers to the place of confessing their sin and trusting Christ to save them. That is the starting place. They have to be carefully grounded in their faith and challenged to a deep concern for souls and a close walk with Christ. They have to be encouraged to taste the heady fruit of witnessing and pointing others to the Saviour and of patiently shepherding the new or weak brother into a strong, vital relationship with Christ. In short, they have to be enlisted as disciples.

Youth Evangelism

The high school group is a fertile mission field. Approximately 80% are from within the church family, but not all of them have had a personal experience with the Lord Jesus Christ. Some are rebellious. Some are indifferent. Some have slid along on the faith of their parents and their church without ever realizing that they have to make a personal commitment themselves if they are to be saved. And, only a small percentage of those who are from outside the church are believers.

So there is a strong evangelistic thrust throughout the high school program. Evangelism takes place through special events such as the Halloween Party as well as through Bible studies and small groups. No one attends very long before he is presented with the opportunity to trust Christ as his Saviour.

"We're constantly reminding ourselves that we have to give these kids the chance to receive Christ while we have the opportunity," one of the youth workers says. "We have them such a brief time we can't afford to waste it."

Every month there are those who come to Christ. The ones who thrill Larmour the most, however, are those who have been reached by their friends of the same age on a one-to-one basis. And this happens with increasing regularity.

Not long ago one of the staff workers had a call from a high school guy. "I wonder if you'd have some material I can give to my buddy," he said. "I helped him receive Christ yesterday. He doesn't know anything about the Bible though. I want to help him all I can."

It excites Larmour to have fellows and girls in high school experiencing the joy of sharing Christ with friends and seeing them make decisions for the Lord. He feels that's evidence of real discipleship.

Even though it would be simpler for Larmour and his adult sponsors to plan the details of the high schoolers' programs and social events, he insists that the kids do it. It takes a certain amount of grace to spend an hour with young people to accomplish something the adults could do in 15 minutes. Still, there would be no learning, no growth in that area, if everything was done for them.

The young people elect their own officers. Through them and the appointed committees, they take care of practically every detail involved in their various activities. They even work on the follow-up of new people and those who have quit coming for some reason.

"It's surprising how much more they can do in this department than we can," the youth pastor admits. "The kids will listen to each other when they probably wouldn't hear a word we say."

"We try to go out on visitation every week," one girl in the group explains, "but we don't make it. I suppose we average about every other week."

The cabinet of the high school group meets on Wednesday nights before the regular meeting. The committees get together afterward.

Making Disciples

Helping the kids meet their spiritual needs and training them for leadership are important requisites for the task of recruiting and training disciples. Larmour sees the task of making disciples as his primary purpose at Redwood Chapel.

"I'm sure my philosophy in this regard is no different from that of the pastor or anyone else on the staff," Larmour says. "I'm convinced that our chief responsibility is that of training kids to do the work of witnessing. If we can get them to make personal contact with others their age, either to share Christ with them or to encourage and build them up in their faith, we're going to accomplish a great deal more than we ever could alone."

In an effort to reach that goal Larmour has a number of discipleship groups in which committed kids seek to know more about God and serving Him. These groups aren't aimed at reaching vast numbers, but at taking a small, hand-picked group who are dedicated enough to make a certain amount of personal sacrifice.

For example, a group of college men meets at 6 o'clock on Thursday mornings. "I like them to meet early because it makes it more difficult for the guys to get there," Larmour says. "It takes an effort to pile out of bed at 5:30 or earlier in order to get over to the place where we're meeting. If a fellow would rather stay in bed, we won't be seeing much of him. We need dedicated guys or the whole program falls apart."

Altogether about 40 kids are involved in three discipleship groups. Larmour would like a limit of 12 for each group and would prefer to have no more than 8 or 10, but one class has 20. They meet for a period of six months.

College-age guys take over the two high school groups. It provides good training for them and also is a help to the fellows of high school age. It does something for them to have a college guy who really loves the Lord care enough about them to spend his time teaching them.

One of the boys, Geoff Way, has come up through the discipleship program. He was in a high school group and when he went on to college he became involved with the older guys. His ability and personal dedication grew.

"He came back to help us as an intern on the staff in the summer of 1974," Don Larmour says. "Geoff's an outstanding student and an unbelievable administrator. Wherever he goes or whatever he does, he's going to make an effective witness for Christ. We're certainly thankful for him and for any part our discipleship program may have had in his development."

College-age Youth

The regular Wednesday night meetings for the college group are also Bible studies. They are conducted somewhat differently than the high school studies, however. The group divides into three discussion classes, each of which is led by one member.

"They are older and more mature," one of the staff relates, "and they have more experience in governing themselves and their activities. We have fewer problems with them, for those reasons, than we have with the high schoolers. It is important for these older young people to direct their own activities. They learn by planning their programs and working out the details. They even run their own discipleship group. Larmour teaches them but they do everything else."

A three-week seminar is held for them during the summer. It is a concentrated period of Bible teaching, which strives to get to the basic problems of edification and Christian growth. There are usually some unsaved who have been brought by friends in the hope that they will be reached for Christ. So the meetings usually include the way of salvation. The main thrust, however, is directed at building up the believers.

At this writing, the youth pastor was quite concerned about the college group. Of the 80 he was working with, 20 or so were dedicated believers, concerned with reaching their peers for Christ. Out of this group came his discipleship class for that age bracket. Another 10 were not so zealous but were still above average. They seemed to have a concern for the things of God but the press of school or their part-time jobs, or personal matters hindered their fullest involvement. Of the 50 or so remaining, 20 more could be counted on to attend the meetings regularly and would do what they were asked to do.

"The rest have their names on the rolls and come whenever they feel like it," he says. "They either aren't believers or have no spiritual depth. We don't have a lot of dropouts, but I'm afraid we're not meeting the needs of those on the fringe. I'm looking forward to the day when we get a good wide-awake young fellow to work with these older kids. It would be a tremendous ministry."

Youth and Missions

The Youth Department takes an active part in the week-long Missions Conference held every year at Redwood Chapel. The guys and gals are encouraged to come in and talk with the missionaries. In order to attract their attention and get them in, Don Larmour and Pastor Williams have tried a variety of schemes. One of the most successful was a series of fireside chats with missionaries in different homes. The hostess would serve a Coke or glass of fruit juice and a cookie or piece of cake to the kids when they came to visit with the missionaries.

They have also held potluck dinners, at which four or five kids would sit at a table with one missionary, giving them an opportunity to get personally acquainted with him and the area where he works. They learned what was going on in his mission field and had the chance to ask the questions that came to their minds.

In April or May the youth have a missions emphasis of their own in the form of a "Slave Day." This is held after the missions conference. The kids select a project from the Church Missions Committee and set about to raise money for it. They work for a couple of dollars an hour and contribute what they earn to the project. In 1973 they raised over half of the $1,200 the Chapel agreed to give to a missionary couple for the purpose of buying a four-wheeled vehicle for use on the field.

One of the young men of the discipleship program completely organized the entire Slave Day project. He found the jobs, lined up the kids and made the assignments so they could go to work.

Though the methods have differed from year to year the purpose has always been the same. The leaders try to spark an interest in missions that will stay with the young people all their lives. The approach is definitely one of a "soft sell," but the ultimate goal has been to challenge young people to consider the mission field as the place of service where God might call them.

As an expression of support for those from the congregation who do respond to the call of missions, the church assumes up to 60% of their financial needs if they have been members four years or more. The church pledges a lesser amount for those who have been members for a shorter time, depending on the length of time they have belonged there. Pastor Williams and the board feel it is good for their missionary candidates to get some prayer and financial support from sources outside Redwood Chapel but they also want them to know the Chapel is solidly behind them.

A number of young people from the church are on various mission fields. Others are in various stages of preparation. One is a missionary intern with Greater Europe Mission. Another couple is in Oklahoma completing training before going into missionary aviation. A single young man is back at Redwood Chapel working as an intern in the Youth Department. No one could say with certainty what actually brought each to his decision, but the important thing is that the program of the Chapel is vital enough to challenge young people to serve Him.

"We proclaim Him, counseling and teaching everyone with all wisdom, so that we may present everyone perfect in Christ" (COL. 1:28).

5

Youth Activities Plus

"I didn't have much use for the church back in the fall of 1970," Rick Reed, a quiet, well-mannered young man in his early 20s, says. "My name was on the membership list of one of the Castro Valley churches, but I didn't go any more often than I had to. Our minister was really an odd ball. The guys used to make fun of him. There wasn't any use in listening to his sermons. We had seen the same news commentators on TV and read the same articles in *Reader's Digest*.

"I probably wouldn't even have gone to the Halloween Party the Redwood Chapel put on that night if the kids in school hadn't been so excited about it. Everybody—but everybody—was going. No one would say much about it except that it was the scariest place in California. By the time we were to meet at the church, I'd have crawled to get there. I was that excited.

"They hauled us over to this place, a bus load at a time, and took us through the building. I knew it wasn't for real, but wow! I thought I'd jump out of my skin! It was a panic!

"Then they took us into one main room. I was beginning to get uptight—like now they had me trapped and were going to give me the business. I felt like splitting, but a lot of kids from my own high school were there. That kind of made me feel at home.

"The big room was packed. I didn't know there were so many kids in Castro Valley. A group of singers gave us a couple of numbers that were really cool, even if they were religious. Then this Johnny MacArthur fellow got up to speak.

"Wow! He was neat! He didn't sound like any preacher I'd ever heard. I didn't believe he was a preacher at first. He used words a guy could understand. And when he talked about God, he came through loud and clear.

"The more he talked about God, the stronger this weird feeling inside of me became. It's sort of hard to describe exactly how I felt. It seemed as if everyone else in the room had disappeared. I didn't even think about the guy who was speaking. It was just God and me.

"When MacArthur asked if any of us wanted to accept Jesus Christ as our personal Saviour, man, I was ready. About 50 other kids were, too. He didn't ask us to come forward. We couldn't have without stepping on a couple of dozen other people. Instead of that he took us into another room to talk to us. Only they didn't have nearly enough people to help with that. I guess they didn't expect so many. Anyway, three of us guys got together without a counselor. We just kind of got to rapping about God. That was really neat."

Associate Pastor Neal Doty picked up the idea of an annual Halloween Party from a friend who was youth minister at a church in the southern part of the state. His friend may have gotten the idea from Youth for Christ, or perhaps the situation was reversed. The important thing is that it worked. For the first such party, in 1970, the planners didn't know how many to expect, and they only had one bus to haul the kids from the church to the Masonic Temple, where they had rented space for the event.

"It was a bit hairy," Doty says. "We expected 150 at the most and 250 showed up. But we got them all there and through the spook house. It went over better than we could have hoped.

"Then MacArthur got up to speak. He is a former football player with a quick sense of humor and had the kids rolling in the aisles. Or he would have if there had been room enough. There were wall-to-wall kids as 250 packed into the space allotted them.

"One in five responded to the invitation," Doty recalls. "It was amazing. MacArthur thought they hadn't understood and went over the way of salvation again. Then he told them that if they really meant it when they held up their hands, they should make their way to the back door and into the room across the hall. The whole bunch—all 50 of them—fought their way over that mass of bodies to get to the door. It was fantastic."

Rick Reed had been one of them. He went on into the Sunday School and youth group. It wasn't long until he was elected president of the high school junior class. The following year he became president of the High School Department.

"And the year after that, when I got into the college group, I was again elected president," he recalls. "But that's not all that's happened to me. In college I became the captain of the track team and the cross country team. This was something new for me. Up until the time I gave my heart to Jesus Christ I was really nobody. All of a sudden I wasn't afraid of people any more. I could meet them without getting all shook up. I couldn't believe the things that were happening, or that they happened so quickly. God made the difference."

He paused.

"I've worked on quite a few Halloween parties since I became a Christian and got active at the Chapel. I'm sold on that method of getting the unchurched kids to come out."

The Halloween party is not an end in itself. It is the kickoff event for an evangelistic effort that continues through the following Sunday morning and evening and Monday through Wednesday nights. On Tuesday night there is a men's fellowship dinner. One of the local football teams and the cheerleaders are invited.

"The last Senior High Halloween party entertained 450 kids on a Friday night. A smaller group showed up for the Junior High Halloween party," a staff member says. "We've never equaled the number of converts of 1970 since but the results have always been gratifying. Those who receive Christ at the party are fed spiritually the next few days in the special meetings. We use other means of follow-up, as well, but those meetings give the new converts a good start."

The Christian kids who are acquainted with the converts are urged to follow up with them. They try to get the new believers into Bible studies, usually on a one-to-one basis. It not only helps the Christians by getting them involved in working with others, but it also strengthens those who have just made a commitment.

The method isn't perfect. There are kids who take the names of new converts and never really follow through with them. Others give up too easily. Still, most of those who make decisions and are uncommitted to another church come into closer fellowship with Christ at the Redwood Chapel. Often, even though the person doing the follow-up may fail, another kid or one of the staff takes over and gets the new Christian working in the many-faceted program of the church so he has opportunity to grow.

Don Larmour, who became Youth Pastor when the press of other duties made it necessary for Neal Doty to give up his duties in that area describes his impressions of the Halloween party as follows:

"We always have kids from other churches who receive Christ at the Halloween party but don't come to any other meetings or activities here at the Chapel, but we actually add eight or ten new converts to our own youth group as a result of the Halloween affair."

Often the party is only the bait that brings the young person in touch with the church and its program. There are always those who make no decision, but because of the party get interested in Redwood Chapel. Some are attracted to the Sunday School, a Bible study, the regular youth program, or even the church worship service, and it is through one of those ministries they are converted.

"This is the thing that makes the TOTAL CHURCH PROGRAM so valuable," says Larmour. "Regardless of how an individual first comes into contact with the church, there are a variety of programs to hold his interest and to bring him face to face with the Person of the Lord Jesus Christ."

Something for Everybody

With any youth group a strong social program seems imperative. In that, Redwood Chapel is no different from the average alert, aggressive church. The wide range of activities there includes something to appeal to everybody.

With the beginning of the football season the first weekend of the school year, there are social times in the gym after the high school football games. Fifth Quarter, as the event is called, provides a rousing good time, followed by refreshments and a devotional. It provides something for the kids to do after games besides tooling around the freeways in their cars. "If there isn't a game we try to have some other kind of a party," the Youth Pastor explains, "so there is something for the kids almost every week." Later in the year interchurch basketball and volley ball leagues help keep numbers of the kids interested in the church. And, beginning with a snow trip at Christmas, the young people take several ski trips into the nearby mountains.

"We've got five kids right now who won't have anything to do with any other program of the church," Larmour says, "but they love to ski. We get them to go along with us when we go into the hills. Even though they just tolerate the Bible studies and devotional times we have while we're there, they are getting the Gospel. As long as they come we have an opportunity to reach them."

About graduation time the church has a formal banquet for the seniors. It rivals the Senior Ball without the dancing. Special singing groups and speakers are featured. This banquet has gradually become one of the top annual events and, second only to the Halloween Party, is looked forward to from one year to the next.

A few years ago the graduation banquet coincided with a Bible Conference Redwood Chapel was having, and those planning the banquet took advantage of that fact using both the speaker and the singer.

"Our radio ensemble, Chapel Singers, and a small orchestra furnished the music for the 45-minute segment of Camelot we were doing," Pastor Neal Doty told us. "Joe [Linn, Minister of Music] took the part of King Arthur. Flo Price, who was singing at the Bible Conference, played the part of Guinevere, and I was Lancelot. We were all in costume, including the choir. The kids fell apart, laughing."

One woman was so interested in the banquet she made all the costumes.

The conference speaker, Dr. Howard Hendricks, brought a message on love. He talked with the kids about the importance of setting up their lives according to God's plan in regard to choosing a life partner.

Some of the kids complained because the church regularly chose the night of the Senior Ball as the time for the banquet, saying it wasn't fair. That did not cause the church to change, however. And even those who protested the loudest still preferred the graduation banquet. In some cases, where parental pressure was strong in that direction, the kids attended the ball. Still, they came to the banquet first. Any time that was left was for the school function.

Summer Explosion

"We try to have activities for the kids all year," the youth pastor relates, "but our program really explodes in the summer. We regularly have three or four times as many programs going on during summer vacation as we do during the school term. You see, 80% of our kids don't work during the summer. It's imperative that we have something interesting for them to do."

The activities vary widely. Christian guys and gals who have been especially trained for it, minister in five-day clubs to kids who have never heard the Gospel of Jesus Christ. There is also bowling, camp, summer seminars, and backpacking trips into the mountains. There is something happening for everyone.

"For an eight-week period last summer we had something the kids could do every single day," a staff member recalls. "We are all agreed that just filling up the spare time of the kids would be important enough to make it practical. And, of course, we try to challenge them for Jesus Christ and lead believers to a new spiritual maturity."

Every year the Youth Department, in cooperation with the Minister of Music, Joseph Linn, sends a group of high schoolers on tour. An itinerary is arranged, lining up a number of churches where they put on a musical program.

"We use kids as ushers and counselors, as well as to sing in the choir, and we always have two or three testimonies in every service," the youth minister says. "In fact, they do just about everything except bring the message. I do that."

A girl, who is now in Bible school, describes her duties as an usherette: "We had to do just about everything. We saw to it that the outfits of the girls who sang were pressed; we took the offering and tried to make sure that everything went smoothly."

She went on to say that she once had the privilege of counseling with a girl who came to Christ as a result of the program. "We wrote to each other for a couple of years," she relates. "The last I heard from her she was going on with Christ in a great way."

One of the boys mentioned the greatest thrill of his several tours. "It was a couple of years ago," he said. "I gave my testimony at one of the meetings, and a guy came to Christ because of it. He didn't tell me, but I heard about it through the kid who counseled with him."

At one of the meetings where the choir sang, a man who hadn't been to church in 16 years rededicated his life to Christ. He was a believer but something had happened to turn him against the church. Soon he had grown cold and indifferent to the things of God.

"Not long after that he went to be with the Lord," Mr. Linn says. "We were all thrilled when we heard how God had used our group to meet that fellow's need and bring him back to Christ."

"Yes," Pastor Williams says, "we have had 50 or more decisions for Christ as a result of our summer youth tours. And, what is just as important, if not more so, is the change those trips have made in the hearts and lives of the participants. Some are going to be soul-winners as long as they live because of the challenge they received on a tour. It's been an encouraging thing to see."

Though many of the high school gang have been reluctant to take High Mountain Encounter, the backpack trip into the hills, those who have gone are enthusiastic about it. Thirty guys made the trip in 1973. A short time later 15 girls went, carrying their 35-pound packs the same as the boys.

"It was rugged," Sharon Lambton, now a student at Moody Bible Institute, says: "One of our guides was a professional mountain climber and a member of a rescue team in the San Bernardino mountains. I know it was a strain for the poor guy to be stopping every five minutes or so to let us rest, but it was an experience that meant a lot to me. All the girls were Christians and we had time to be alone with God, to allow Him to talk to our hearts. I'm sure some very important decisions were made on that trip."

The boys' trip attracted a number of unchurched guys. Some were like the five mentioned earlier who enjoyed skiing but wouldn't get involved in any of the rest of the church programs. They went along only because they were anxious to make the hike. The Christian emphasis was something they would have to endure.

"Some of them figured we were pansies because we are Christians," one young man who made the trip related. "But when they got on the mountain with us and went 2,000 feet straight up it sort of changed their ideas."

Four of the unbelievers who made the trip in 1973 came back with changed lives. They had met Jesus Christ on the mountain.

The girls use professional guides from the Park Service. The same help was offered to the guys but they turned it down. A couple of fellows in the church who knew the area quite well went with them instead.

"That was a lot more fun," one of the boys remembers. "We'd go about a thousand feet up a cliff and turn a corner. And, wow! There was nothing there! We'd have to go all the way down and find another route to the top.

"We thought we knew the exact trail but we got lost every once in awhile. It was neat!

"Before we left Castro Valley, Don [Larmour] told us we were supposed to stretch ourselves spiritually the way we stretched ourselves physically. We learned a lot about doctrine and what a man of God should know. I guess we were really learning specific things the Bible says."

Every night when they made camp there was an hour or so of Bible study. No scheduled time was set for ending the study. They continued until they understood the passage or until it got too dark to read.

"It's a good time and place to study the Word," the youth pastor observes. "We've had some exciting decisions made on those trips."

Changes were made in High Mountain Encounter in 1974. Though the program had been successful the few years it had been in operation, it was decided to take a mixed group of college age young people into the hills.

"We had a number of reasons for wanting to make the change," the youth pastor says. "With the proper chaperones we knew we would have no problems we couldn't handle, and putting the boys and girls together has definite advantages.

"Some of the guys were in excellent physical condition and were used to climbing. They could strike out as though they were walking to the corner drugstore or to the nearest supermarket. Others were out of shape and couldn't keep up. They were razzed so much they didn't want to go again.

"With a mixed group, we figured that if some fellows did lag behind, plenty of girls would be going slower too, so they wouldn't be alone. In fact the eager beavers would probably slow up to some extent. And we thought that combining the two groups would increase interest."

It did. Just about everybody signed up to make the 1974 trip.

From 90 to 100 high schoolers and 30 to 40 from junior high go to camp from Redwood Chapel during the summer. The church does not operate a camp for its own program but sends young people to the Hume Lake Conference Grounds where they share in the regular camping program with young people from all over California. In all 800 kids attend.

The activities are somewhat like those at the Chapel in that they are varied enough to maintain the interest of a vigorous, lively crowd. Mornings are devoted to study. Afternoons are planned to siphon off as much extra energy as possible and wear the kids out so they will find it easier to listen and take part in the evening study sessions.

"We appreciate the care with which the program is put together," Larmour told us. "We want to be sure our kids are challenged for Christ, but it's possible to bore even the most devout with too much Bible and not enough outside activity. It takes an intelligent balance to do the best job."

"So whether you eat or drink or whatever you do, do it all for the glory of God" (1 COR. 10:31).

6

The Ministry of Music

Joseph Linn came to Redwood Chapel as the Minister of Music on a part-time basis in 1963, the first staff member to assist Pastor Williams. He already lived in the area and was attending college nearby, but Redwood Chapel was not his home church.

"I really didn't know too much about it," he recalls. "I attended a small church in the valley and had never even been to a service at Redwood Chapel. All I knew about the church was what I heard from 'Sherry' [now Mrs. Martin Erickson], Sherm's daughter. I'd been working with her in Youth for Christ. She recommended me to her dad. I was interviewed and got the job."

Linn thought of it as a beginning, an opening into the field of Christian music, where he was convinced God was calling him to serve. He would gain experience at Redwood

91

Chapel which would look good on his record when he graduated from college and set out to find a full-time position. He has been at Redwood Chapel ever since; half-time at first, then three-quarters of the time, and finally full-time.

The Music Department operates on the same TOTAL CHURCH PROGRAM concept as every other department. It took some time to reach that place, but today Joe Linn has a full complement of choirs and vocal and instrumental groups. The vocal music program starts with grade three and goes up to the adults, who have two sections of the Chapel Choir, one for each of the two Sunday morning services. The adults also have two special select groups for use on their radio and television programs.

Instrumentalists don't start quite as young as the vocalists. They begin with grades five and six, though not on a regular basis. Linn assembles and arranges what he needs for a particular occasion among the kids of this age.

There are a number of brass, rhythm, and string groups among the older fellows and girls, including a Junior High Orchestra, and the same variety of groups as among the adults.

"Most musicians, Christian or otherwise, groan when anyone mentions a church orchestra," Neal Doty says frankly. "And we've got to admit that most of them are far from what they should be, musically. But we don't have to make apologies for any of our groups, especially our studio orchestra. A lot of the guys are professionals or are heading in that direction. Believe me, they're terrific."

Linn is a professional musician with the ability to recognize superior talent and train it effectively. "I guess we just like to play for him," one young man comments.

One of Linn's groups accompanies the Bill Gaither family when they are making appearances nearby. He also arranged instrumental groups to accompany the well-known Gospel singer Norman Nelson in his three most recent recordings.

Gaither used to get together a group of his own or bring in musicians from Southern California, where he makes his home, before he learned what Linn can do. After using the Redwood Chapel brass for one concert, he was so well satisfied he no longer concerns himself with arranging for accompanying musicians for their San Francisco-Oakland concerts. He calls Linn and turns the responsibility over to him.

"I've had offers to go other places," Linn acknowledges. "Most of the fellows in the music field do, if they have anything on the ball. But it's great serving the Lord here at Redwood Chapel. I am happy to stay right here as long as the Lord can use me."

Pastoral Relations

Joe Linn went on to speak of the wisdom and kindness shown him by Pastor Williams, especially when he first started to work at Redwood Chapel. "I came here as a kid with no experience to speak of and a bag full of plans and new ideas. Some of them were good but some were terrible. Pastor Williams guided me so graciously in discarding my stupid plans and adopting those with merit that I will never forget it.

"Take the time I came in to talk with him about using the guitar in some of the services, for example. He was a little older than I, so I assumed he was prejudiced against any instrument except the organ and the piano. I worked up a lengthy discourse on what the guitar could do and why it should be used. He listened to me as intently as though he had never heard of the instrument before but was intrigued by what I was telling him. Several years later I learned that he was accomplished on the guitar himself. Indeed, he had probably forgotten more about the instrument than I had ever learned. But he let me talk him into allowing the guitar to be used occasionally. I'm sure he kept quiet about his own expertise with it because he didn't want to embarrass me. That is typical of him.

"Knowing of my inexperience and youth, he guided me into my duties with a gentle hand. As I gained in understanding of how he wanted things done and developed more confidence in myself, he gradually allowed me to take over. I assumed more and more of the responsibilities until finally I was carrying the full load of the Music Department.

"It's been the same with each member of the staff. As quickly as he can, Pastor Williams allows us free reign. We know that as long as we keep the best interests of the work at heart he is going to see that we have the authority to carry out our responsibilities."

Another member of the staff mentions the same trait in Williams. "He knows everything that's going on and is sure that we are working in accord with the guidelines that have been provided us, but ours is a team effort. We don't have the feeling that we are working under a boss and must do everything he says. We're part of the staff and our efforts are to the glory of God. You can't imagine what a difference that makes in our morale and unity of spirit."

Music as Outreach

A different philosophy governs the younger age musical groups than the others. Those made up of younger kids are an outreach in themselves, ministering to the unchurched parents and their children as well as to those who listen. For this reason there is no requirement of salvation or even Sunday School or church attendance for those who take part.

"We've got a lot of kids in my wife's groups who are completely outside the church," Linn says. "They seldom come to any kind of a service. I think the reason some of the parents have their kids in our musical groups is for the free training they get. But we don't mind that. We use the kids in a service and the parents will come to hear their kids sing. They get the Gospel at the same time and are exposed to the friendliness and warmth of the church. We've had some thrilling stories of families who have been reached for Christ because a son or daughter began to sing in our Music Makers group."

The same policy is followed through the junior high level, with good results. For example, the parents of Kim and Jodi Vogel were members of another church but felt they were doing well if they attended services at Christmas and Easter. Their children got involved in the Redwood Chapel program, however, and received Christ shortly before they went into junior high school and became eligible for Teen Tones.

Their parents were glad for the musical training and were quite willing to have them sing in the services at church. In fact they would attend on those occasions, themselves. Still, they were reluctant to have Kim and Jodi sing with the group outside the church such as at hospital services.

"I think I know why they didn't want the kids to go out with us," Linn says, "but I'm not sure. When we urged Kim and Jodi to come with us and talked with their parents about it, however, they decided to let them take part. In fact, it wasn't long until Mr. and Mrs. Vogel began to take an interest themselves. They started to travel with us on the junior high singing engagements to help us. Finally they began to see their own need of the Lord Jesus Christ as their personal Saviour. They accepted Him and made a total commitment of their lives to God. Now they're practically indispensable in our junior high program. I don't know what I'd do without them."

Of 125 in the junior high youth group, 50 or more are involved in the musical activities. Called Teen Tones, the junior high choir and orchestra is the training ground for vocalists and instrumentalists in the church.

"Kids of this age are usually getting active in the public school musical program," the Minister of Music explains. "If we can get them into our program at this age, we can train them to use their abilities in music to worship God, to witness to unbelievers, and to be an encouragement to other Christians. We started Teen Tones three years ago and we've been excited with the results."

Though the junior high groups do not take long tours such as those involving the high school and college groups, they do go to nearby churches and to other parts of Northern California close enough to make in one-day trips. They also go to convalescent hospitals and homes for the aged in addition to taking part in the services at the Chapel.

Music as Ministry

With the senior high kids, policy changes. Linn expects them and those in the college and adult groups to be believers. "We don't require church membership," he says, "but how can anyone sing of the love of God with authority if he has never experienced that love?

"We have, on rare occasions, made exceptions to this rule, but only in cases where there was such a keen interest in the Lord Jesus Christ that we felt allowing the person to sing would be a factor in bringing him to the place where he would receive Christ."

According to Linn, he is not really concerned about having a choir of people who possess great talent and technical skill. He wants people who have a personal relationship with Jesus Christ and who want to sing to His honor and glory, communicating the message of Christian love.

"Our responsibility is to minister," he declares. "We have to use the people who can do that best. We have some excellent musicians who can't understand why they aren't used more. They can't seem to communicate effectively. They can't seem to use their voices to influence people to listen more intently to the pastor, or to help someone reach a decision in his own life. Regardless of their abilities, if they can't present the message of Christ in a way that will speak to hearts, we can't use them very often."

Another musical group in the long list of choirs, ensembles, and instrumentalists at Redwood Chapel is the Freedom Singers, made up of those in the college and career age bracket.

"We aren't primarily interested in musical ability for the Freedom Singers," Alan Bishop, the director of that group, says. "And we don't make attendance at our 9 to 10 o'clock practice sessions on Wednesday night mandatory. We simply wanted to give them a chance to express their faith."

Working with youth pastor Don Larmour, who had been in on its development from the beginning, the Freedom Singers planned a short tour in May and June of 1974. There were 30 singers with a four-piece brass and rhythm section. The program began and ended with music. A short segment in the middle featured testimonies.

"I hope the program was edifying to the audience," Larmour says, "but I *know* what it did for those taking part. Frankly, I was amazed by the effect it had on both the fellows and girls. It taught me that music is a vital force in spreading the Gospel and challenging people to holy living, and especially for those who sing or play." Typical of the testimonies given by the Freedom Singers is the following, of one of the girls:

"I don't know how long I've been searching for a place to worship where Christianity is real and vital in the lives of the people. I started to come to Redwood Chapel because of the musical opportunities it afforded. God has been working in my life through the Sunday School in a way I'd never have dreamed possible. Now, I can share my faith through the medium of music."

Another girl, Shirley, came into the group because she wanted to sing, not because proclaiming Christ meant a great deal to her. She was a believer but was very weak. It wasn't long until she was actively sharing Christ with those she met.

John had a similar experience. He wasn't much of a singer. He admitted it. But it was something to do and he had a gnawing emptiness inside. Not long after he began to sing with the Freedom Singers, he rededicated his life to Christ.

Musical Sidelights

Linn has had some interesting experiences in locating musicians for special purposes. On one occasion he was putting together a group for a recording session with a quartette. Everyone was lined up except a guitarist. He had not been able to find anyone who could play well enough for recording.

"Then a fellow came to our door to collect for our insurance," he says. "I'd gone to school with him for a short time and he had dated my wife before we were married. He wasn't attending church at all, but he was an excellent guitarist. He had been doing a lot of rock 'n' roll and country music.

"I made contact with him and suggested that he help us. We spent an entire day recording. It wasn't a top project by any means but it was a lot of fun."

The spirit of the guys he was playing with and their testimonies got to the guitarist. "I've never been in a group like this, Joe," he said. "Every other time I've been in on a recording session it's been a real hassle."

A month later Linn used the same guitarist to record a

Christmas album with Norman Nelson. The recording was done on a Saturday, and they spent all day in the studio. The guitarist was supposed to play at an all-night party, starting at 10 o'clock that same evening. He was there for an hour when he got sick and had to leave. The next morning he came to church. Two weeks later Joe invited him to go to the Overseas Crusades Conference where Redwood Chapel instrumental and vocal groups would accompany Nelson.

The following Friday night, Joe Linn invited him to play at a meeting where Bill McKee was speaking. The guitarist became a Christian that night. Since then he has given up rock 'n' roll, has written many beautiful Gospel songs, and is a vital part of Redwood Chapel's instrumental program.

The Studio Orchestra, The Revised Edition, and the Chapel Singers are the most professional groups in the Music Department. They were originated to meet the exacting demands of television and radio. The orchestra is made up of professionals or those who are looking to a career in music and want to use their talents in that area. The Chapel Singers and The Revised Edition are gleaned from the best voices in both sections of the Chapel Choir.

"Those musical groups have much to do with the success of our television ministry," Neal Doty, who is in charge of the radio and television outreach says. "And they've been an excellent advertisement for our church. I'm sure they have been responsible for some of the growth of Redwood Chapel."

"Let the word of Christ dwell in you richly as you teach and counsel one another with all wisdom, and as you sing psalms, hymns, and spiritual songs with gratitude in your hearts to God" (COL. 3:16).

7

The Local Church
on Radio and Television

It was almost inevitable that Redwood Chapel would go into some type of communications outreach once Neal Doty joined the staff. He had gone to the California church from Moody Bible Institute's radio network, where he had been a producer for three years. He was sold on using the airwaves as a means of evangelism and church promotion.

The Chapel's first effort was a radio program on a local Christian station. But they looked beyond radio to television. The newest building in the Redwood Chapel complex was designed with space for a control room. Conduit for cable runs was placed in the floor.

"Actually," Doty says, "we had a physical facility that would provide for production of anything from a one-man phone show to a basketball game or live drama."

A decision was made to purchase production equipment

and to seek time on the local cable television system. When the local cable company learned of these plans, they approached the Chapel about producing material for a local channel. They weren't doing any production of their own at the time and were eager to get some programs that originated in the immediate area.

"We were quick to take advantage of the opportunity," Pastor Williams recalls. "And why wouldn't we? After a certain amount of negotiation Redwood Chapel was offered the opportunity to make the message of Christ available to the 6,000 subscriber homes without cost, except for equipment."

Nothing related to television is inexpensive. The first purchase of equipment totaled $50,000 and included three black-and-white cameras, two videotape recorders, and associated controls and lighting.

Doty became the station manager of Chanel 12B, and set about to build up a schedule of good programs. At this writing, Redwood Chapel is on the air with 50 hours a week of live and taped programs.

"We've just received a new piece of equipment that will make it posible for us to greatly increase our air time," the associate pastor said. "We won't be able to do that immediately but will gradually add programming.

"We're able to air color tapes now and will soon be able to use color films. Eventually we hope to purchase color cameras in order to be able to produce our own color programming. Now we rent a color TV camera truck for all Sunday telecasting."

Dr. Bruce Dunn, pastor of the Grace Presbyterian Church of Peoria, Ill. was the speaker for the Redwood Chapel Bible Conference in 1973. He was so impressed with the television ministry and the possibilities of witness through cable TV that he went home and raised $100,000 to buy cameras and equipment for the same sort of project. He now has Channel 13 in Peoria.

Why Get into TV?

"A lot of Christians misunderstand our purpose for the station," Doty said. "A few days ago someone from a large church in the San Francisco area called to ask us about it. The first thing the caller wanted to know was how many people it had brought into the church. Our growth pattern is such that we are not all that concerned about packing as many people as possible into the Chapel. We've just started a second branch church because we were at capacity again. Now we're headed in the same direction again. Our goal is to reach people who either can't, or won't, come to church. We believe they will feel more a part of a local service than they would be in watching Rex Humbard, for example, even though his program packaging is much more professional than ours."

"Television is a tool for getting the Gospel before people who have no use for the church," Pastor Williams explains. "It has become a most successful form of outreach. Two-thirds of the people who subscribe to cable TV in Castro Valley have actually watched one of our programs."

One of the first to be reached by the Chapel's venture into television was not a viewer but a construction worker who attended services occasionally. Though he had never made a decision for Christ, he got into a home Bible study and participated in a special TV taping with Dr. Howard Hendricks. One day he approached the associate pastor with tears in his eyes.

"I've been coming to church here off and on for a long time but I must not've been listening to anything that was said. I really didn't know what this Christianity bit is all about until a few weeks ago. I've decided to give my life to Christ."

Shortly afterward he began to operate a TV camera for Channel 12B regularly.

Sunday services at Redwood Chapel are telecast live. "We haven't made any changes in the format of the meetings," Neal Doty says. "We've just added lights and cameras. A lot of people seem to think we've streamlined the program to make it move more rapidly, but we haven't.

"What we do can best be explained this way. The camera is a spectator. We put it out in the audience—or I should say we put three of them in the auditorium among the people and let them record what is going on.

"In other types of programming the camera is creative. It paces the program, creating interest with novel angles, interesting scenes, and so on. It is actually a vital part of production. But for our purpose the spectator camera is by far the most suitable. We want the people outside to know what our services are like. Actually, we want to transport them to church by means of the telecast."

Many who have never been to a service in Redwood Chapel still consider it their church. They claim it because they attend by television every Sunday. A woman in her 70s was like that. She was confined to her home with a severe heart condition but that wasn't the only thing keeping her from church. She had been in a church building only once that she could remember. That was years before when she was selling mausoleum space and went there to talk to a member of the staff.

She had gotten acquainted with one of the secretaries at the Redwood Chapel, however, and liked her very much. One evening she called her friend, somewhat disturbed. "You were supposed to sing in church this morning, but you didn't. Is something wrong?"

"I wasn't feeling well," her friend explained. "But how did you know?"

"Oh, I watch every Sunday morning."

At first the woman watched the program out of curiosity because of her friend who went there and worked on the staff. After a time, however, Redwood Chapel became her church.

"I sit right here and watch every Sunday," she told Pastor Doty when he went to see her after learning of her interest.

It wasn't long until she asked for a Bible. Then she wanted offering envelopes. Finally she trusted Christ as her Saviour and wanted to be baptized. Because of her health, the baptismal service was conducted privately with only the church staff present.

"She was one person we wouldn't have been able to reach in any other way than by television," Doty says.

Varied Programming

"Young Life" is a program Channel 12B has done in the past in cooperation with the youth organization of the same name.

"It was a simple program," Neal Doty says. "We would take a portable TV camera and a tape recorder to the campus and the hangouts around town for high school kids.

"We would ask questions of the kids such as, 'How do you define security?' We sorted out the most interesting responses, edited them, and put them together in the studio. We did a review at the close and wrapped up the program with the conclusion that security really is in Jesus Christ. We put a little music with it and put it on the air."

The program built up a large viewing audience because it featured local high school kids.

"One girl came down here at 9:15 one Saturday morning, dragging her mother with her so they could see the show she was on. They didn't have cable TV at their home, and she was determined not to miss it. She watched the last half of 'Tree House Club,' which is for little kids, and all of 'Young Life.' Twenty minutes into the show, she was on the screen for 30 seconds. That response was a little extreme, but keen interest is typical."

Most of the church's programming is for adults, but they have "Tree House Club" and a daily program, "Black Buffalo's PowWow," for children. They also did a two-hour locally developed children's musical, written and produced by a woman who lived in nearby Walnut Creek.

"It was professionally done in spite of the fact that the people who did it are amateurs," Doty claims. "There were 30 local grade school children and several adults in it, and they had four set changes. They recorded all the audio first, and when they put on a performance, the kids lip-synced their lines and the lyrics to their musical numbers. I don't know that I've ever seen an amateur production with more class."

They came down to the Redwood Chapel and the Channel 12B staff produced the show for television, videotaping it in 10-minute segments and assembling it as they went along. ("We have four video tape recorders now," one of the men explains. "One is a sophicated machine that permits us to do one segment, then do a rolling start and go into the next 10 minutes.") When they got through, they had a finished product ready to go on the air. The entire session took 13½ hours. The kids performed like troupers.

In addition to their own locally produced programs, Channel 12B airs programs such as "Old Time Gospel Hour" from Lynchburg, Va., "Sunday Celebration" from El Dorado Park Community Church in Long Beach, Calif., and "The Bible As It Is," produced by Dr. Harlin J. Roper of Dallas, Texas. In addition they screen "Day of Discovery" with Richard De Haan, and "Encounter" with Dr. Stephen Olford.

Youth groups from other churches come in from time to time to attend "Sunday Nite Sing" a 30-minute variety TV program distributed to other cable TV systems. Occasionally this will include a brief segment called "Dan's Dazzling Ditty." (It use to be called "Marilyn's Mystery Melody.") A Gospel song is played and people are supposed to identify it. If they can, they are given a gift certificate for a frozen creation at a local ice cream parlor.

"It's a fun thing," Doty explains. "We like to air this sort of program to let people know there are Christians who don't act as though they are perpetually in mourning."

"Sunday Nite Sing" is the most professional program produced by the Redwood Chapel teleproduction staff. The 15-piece Studio Orchestra and the Revised Edition vocal group do the opening theme, and there is often a guest musical artist.

"It's a much faster paced program than our Sunday morning services," Doty says, "or anything else we've done. It's tightly planned and each segment is timed as carefully as some network shows. We have five or six musical numbers. I interview our guest and close with a brief sermonette. We make a break midway in the program in case the station wishes to insert a commercial."

"Sunday Night Sing" is now syndicated. At this writing, it is on 14 cable TV stations and three radio stations. Adding new outlets has proved to be very simple. Doty gets more requests than he has been able to take care of with the current staff and budget.

"We've been pleased by the fact that we get letters from 7-year-old kids and people in their 80s telling us they like the program," Doty says.

Some stations have been a bit concerned about the music on the show at times, that it is a little too modern for the taste of their conservative audiences.

"It's not easy to be contemporary and yet not be offensive," Doty admits, "especially when you have a program like ours that's 80% to 85% music." One song particularly concerned Doty. "It was an upbeat number," he recalls. "I liked it myself, but I was concerned about the reaction we might get."

Two days later he had a phone call from an elderly woman in a nursing home in San Jose, California. "I've enjoyed your program so very much," she said, "but I particularly enjoyed that song. I don't have a tape recorder but I'm going to get one. I would like to have a tape of that song so I can play it whenever I want to."

There was other mail about that number, all of it favorable.

"I guess we needn't have been concerned," Doty says. "It was a song that God used in an unusual way on our program. We don't get a lot of mail, but every now and then God lets us have a little peek at what our efforts in radio and television are accomplishing, so we can be encouraged."

"For from you sounded out the Word of the Lord" (1 THES. 1:8, KJV).

8

Special Ministries

Many of the activities inaugurated at Redwood Chapel after Pastor Sherman Williams arrived were brought into being specifically to fill a vacant place in their TOTAL CHURCH PROGRAM. The pastor, his staff, and the board would look at what they were doing and see that something had to be developed for certain age groups in order to provide a program for everyone. Other programs were worked out to insure adequate follow-up for converts of all ages, or to offer leadership and discipleship training.

Some programs, however, could never have been anticipated or worked out by man. They were called into being as God inspired individuals to fill specific needs. The program at the Chapel is flexible enough to provide room for such developments. In fact, Pastor Williams definitely seeks to encourage them.

Alcoholics' Wives

The Bible studies for the wives of alcoholics came into being in just that way. Liz Fosdahl did not decide to start it on her own. It was thrust on her as she learned the need of several of the women in her Sunday School class. They were trying to cope with the havoc alcoholism brings to a home.

She knew all about the ugly shadow of liquor addiction because her mother had recently died from alcoholism.

A little more than a year before, God had miraculously worked in her mother's life. On her deathbed the mother had prayed for forgiveness and to receive Christ as her Saviour. But Liz was deeply concerned for those who were still caught in the trap of despair. She wanted desperately to help them.

And she was not alone. God had been working in the heart of another member of the class, urging her to do something for those in the class who needed this sort of help.

Liz and her friend didn't know for sure what they could do to help. They didn't know enough about all the ramifications of alcoholism to offer sound advice. But they could share their faith. That, and a ready ear.

"We knew Christ could comfort these wives in a special way," Liz said, "and that it helped at times just to have someone to talk to. And we knew that the application of Christian principles, even in a thorny situation like alcoholism, could help by removing some of the irritants that inevitably arise."

The first meeting was not what either of the organizers expected. The women came, but they wanted to talk about their own problems, to air all the hurt and anger and bitterness that surged through their hearts.

"When we had the opportunity, we talked about alcoholic problems from a Christian standpoint," Liz recalls. "And how Christian principles could solve some of these problems. This proved to be the approach we would use in future sessions.

Though we constantly use the Bible, I'm not sure you would call our meetings a Bible study. At least they don't fit in that general pattern."

The get-togethers helped some of the women see the importance of keeping the person of Jesus Christ before them as their standard. If they looked only at their own husbands, bound by liquor and all the problems and difficulties it brings, they came off looking virtuous by comparison. They could almost consider themselves sort of superbeings. Some did just that. It was part of their problem. They couldn't see their own sins because of their husbands' sins.

Once the women began to compare themselves with Christ they saw their own nagging bitterness and hatred. They saw their own spiritual needs. Not all of them, of course. But there were those who confessed their sin and got right with God. The meetings, which are held every other week through the winter months, are a source of strength and help to them.

"I think Christians who are married to alcoholics answer to a higher calling than the rest of us," Mrs. Fosdahl concluded. "It is not until a person is put under a pressure situation that she realizes the Lord is so much greater than she has ever known before. We can praise Him. He is working."

Because of the concern of Mrs. Fosdahl and her friend— and because of a church that encourages its members to act when they see a need—there are women with alcoholic husbands who have found a way of lessening their problems, who enjoy a strength and peace they didn't know was available to them.

Prison Ministry

At least 20 adults from Redwood Chapel are involved in a local prison ministry on a regular basis. Others participate periodically.

The ministry, known as Follow-up Supply Line, was founded by Glenn Morrison, now a member at Redwood. When Glenn was director of Youth For Christ in Oakland, Calif., he was impressed with the need for adequate follow-up materials for those who responded to salvation invitations. He set about to develop a systematic follow-up program and found that the popularity of that program soon spread far beyond usage in Youth For Christ. Servicemen and prison inmates were mailed correspondence courses and soon responses began to come in from around the nation and the world.

As a result of all this, Morrison was invited to hold services in California prisons and juvenile institutions. From this beginning has grown a significant prison ministry that reaches into every prison in California and Nevada, as well as into the local juvenile hall.

Morrison and members of his staff, plus musical groups and individuals from Redwood and other churches, are flown around the state by a Redwood layman who sees his role as one of "giving wings" to the Gospel. This man and many others are also involved in one-to-one witnessing before and after meetings in the prisons and juvenile institutions.

Results have been thrilling, not only with disturbed youngsters but even with hardened men in solitary confinement in prisons such as strife-torn San Quentin. Follow-Up Supply Line people have seen God change lives through their personal concern and sharing of the Word of God.

Bible Studies for the Unsaved

"I think it was Dr. Howard Hendricks who got us started on Bible studies for the unsaved when he was here to speak at one of our Bible Conferences," Neal Doty says. "We get a small group of Christians together and instruct them as to the purpose of our study and the general form it will take. We tell them it is one Bible study to which they aren't coming to learn. It is for their unsaved neighbors. They are not to ask any questions that might confuse an unbeliever."

The Christians are instructed not to come unless they bring an unsaved friend. Doty usually uses the Book of Romans for this series of studies because it presents basic salvation doctrine. The plan is to meet once a week for 10 weeks. Doty has conducted two such series a year.

"In our first study I began by teaching verses 1-16 of the first chapter," the associate pastor remembers. "When I got through, I asked if there were any questions. There was dead silence. For a minute I was floored. I hadn't expected that. Then I asked if they had any other questions to ask about God, whether I had touched on it in the study or not. One girl said, 'How do you know there is a God? Have you ever seen Him?' Then the discussion got lively and profitable.

"I don't know how many have made definite decisions as a result of these particular Bible studies. We haven't prayed with anyone at the meetings. But I'm convinced we're touching hearts."

A number of women's home Bible studies in the area meet regularly every week and are geared to reach non-Christians. "A friend asked me if I would lead a new group to start in our neighborhood," Linda Tatro remembers. "I had been a believer for only two years myself, but I told her I would try if I could get someone to open her home for it. The first person I asked was agreeable.

"These Bible study groups aren't a part of Redwood Chapel," Linda says. "But Pastor Williams has always encouraged us to get involved in serving Christ, regardless of whether the activity is a part of our church or not. We never mention our church or advocate one church above another in our meetings. Yet, from a practical standpoint the subject does come up in private conversations when we are counseling with a woman who is receiving Christ. When a new believer asks me about the church I attend, I tell her about Redwood Chapel. We have a number of women—and even whole families—who are members now because of the Bible studies."

Usually the groups include some who have drifted away from the Lord in addition to non-Christians. They've been invited in by their neighbors. Over a cup of coffee (they serve no food), the women go through the lesson informally. The leader does little more than guide the discussion, keeping it on the lesson and free of controversial doctrine. There are seldom more than eight or ten participants, the number who can gather comfortably around the average kitchen table. Because they provide a baby-sitter in another home, they break up in an hour and a half.

"Our study has been going for a year," Mrs. Tatro says. "We've had two women saved, and six who were out of fellowship with Christ have come back to Him. They hadn't gone to church for 10 or 12 years, but they are attending regularly now."

Though the Bible studies are constantly directed toward salvation, few of those who confess their sin and trust Christ do so in the regular meetings. It is when the Christians talk with them personally during the week that this work is done.

"I'll never forget the first woman I had the privilege of leading to Christ," Mrs. Tatro recalls. "She and her husband were having problems, and she started attending a church not far from her home. Someone there told her she ought to be baptized, so she was baptized and joined the church, though she knew nothing about accepting Jesus Christ as her personal Saviour. She still had not resolved either her spiritual or marital problems. I went to see her one afternoon, after she had been going to our Bible study for awhile, and she received

Christ. That was one of the most exciting days of my life! To think that I had been privileged to help someone else receive the Christ, who had brought such peace and joy to me!"

Home Visitation

The Prayer and Care Group, an organization of the church directed by Mrs. Winston Miller and Mrs. Sherman Williams, meets every Thursday. The women make personal calls on church guests and visitors who live within a 10-mile radius of Redwood Chapel. "From 8 to 15 families visit our church each Sunday," Mrs. Miller says, "and we try to get to them the first week after they have come. Usually 10 or 12 of us do the calling. We go out in pairs. We take along two dozen cookies, a brochure telling about the Redwood Chapel, a *Power* paper, and perhaps a copy of *The Christian Reader.*"

They also have a doorknob hanger so they can leave the packet if no one is home. They get phone calls in return, thanking them and expressing surprise that they called so soon.

The primary purpose of the visitation is to welcome new people to the church. That, according to the women who go out calling for this purpose, is reward enough. When they see a new family begin coming regularly, they can feel that perhaps they had a part in helping them to choose Redwood Chapel.

At least three ladies the group has visited in recent months were led to Christ by those who made the calls. The women expressed an interest in salvation at the initial visit, and the visitors returned to explain in more detail how to receive Christ.

Then there was a man who went forward one Sunday morning. The Prayer and Care women had made a call to his home two weeks before. After they had made a visit, Pastor Williams called on the family. The man had also been approached by the Mormons, who had aroused his curiosity about Christ and the Christian faith. Not long afterward, he responded to the invitation to receive Christ.

"I've had opportunity to observe him in the year and a half since he made his decision," Pastor Williams says, "and there has been a steady spiritual growth."

Food and Fun

The Sweetheart Banquet, a Valentine's Day affair, was never intended to be more than a one-time event when it was started 12 years ago. The women had been cooking for the monthly meetings of the Men's Fellowship all year. As the February meeting approached, the men decided to take their wives out to dinner as a little token of appreciation.

It was so much fun for everyone that the event became a regular yearly affair. However, finding a restaurant to take a group of their size and provide a good meal at a fair price became increasingly difficult. After five years Mrs. Thelma Johnson volunteered to take charge.

"We only had a small chapel that could be used for that purpose at the time," recalls Mrs. Johnson, "but we could seat 224. That was enough to take care of our numbers then."

The meal now is always catered. Seven years ago the tickets sold for $3. In 1974 they were $6 each, and the committee had to cut off ticket sales when the number reached 508. The program is mostly secular music, love songs of the past and present, always with a theme. This leads to the final musical package concerning God's love and our response to Him.

"We have done 'Love Songs Around the World,'" Mrs. Johnson says, "'Love Songs of the Seasons,' and our own version of a musical. We try to keep the theme traditional so we can have costumes. Everybody loves that. One year we used pantomime to act out the lyrics. It went over very well."

Toward the end of the program there is a brief but pointed presentation of the Gospel.

Couples come to the banquet from as far away as 200 miles. Some Christians bring several unsaved couples. "At least 20 people in our church right now were reached through the Sweetheart Banquet," says Mrs. Johnson. "It has been such an effective means of exposing unbelievers to the claims of Christ on their lives that we have considered holding the banquet twice a year."

"I have become all things to all men so that by all possible means I might save some. I do all this for the sake of the Gospel that I may share in its blessings" (1 COR. 9:22-23).

9

Finding
a Better Way

Annual church business meetings can be boring affairs that drone on endlessly. Officers stumble through page after page of reports couched in dull terms and presenting facts few are able to follow and almost nobody recalls once they have been read and accepted. Not so at Redwood Chapel.

"We borrowed an idea from our 1967 Sunday School contest," Sherman Williams explains. "We kept a scrapbook during the contest, which we filled with pictures taken at various activities and events. It created so much interest that we decided to use pictures taken throughout the year to show at our business meetings."

Both stills and movies, the pictures tell the story of the year's activities as fully as possible. Rather than someone reading that the Halloween Party was attended by more than 450 high school kids, for example, a movie shows the kids pushing their way into the building where they will listen to a message after going through the Spook House. Action slides of the Bible studies do more than a thousand words in demonstrating their effectiveness. Pictures of the rapt faces of the younger kids in Children's Church show how they receive the story. The look in a missionary's eyes when he learns the church is going to supply him with a piece of equipment he has been praying about for a year is a powerful tool for selling missions to the congregation.

Overheads, slides, movies—all three are used to tell the story of the year's activities. The segments are carefully integrated. A script is written and narrated on tape. The finished product is a cohesive, fast-moving account that people can enjoy.

"Moreover," Williams points out, "it can be filed away for use in later years." What a tremendous history of their church this will provide.

Reports are read and acted on, just as in any congregation, but they are kept short. Streamlining the business meetings has revitalized them. The pastor no longer has to plead with the people to attend only to be disappointed by a host of vacant chairs.

"Our annual business meetings are very well attended," Neal Doty says. "People know they're not going to be bored out of their minds and that the meeting is going to move along briskly. I think our business meetings are a good example of the vision and creative thinking of Pastor Williams. He's a step or two ahead of everyone else. I'm still amazed by some of the things he does, and I've been on the staff for nine years."

Staff Relations

"I don't want to be critical of some of the other multiple-staff situations I've observed," says Doty, "but some pastors are virtual dictators and the world falls in on anyone who dares to have a different idea about what to do.

"Some wouldn't consider letting their associates preach. I know of men who are almost afraid to take a vacation because they don't want anyone else in that pulpit they've come to think of as their own. They're so insecure that they fear they will lose the church if the people get an opportunity to hear anyone else. Pastor Williams isn't that way.

"For example. I preach on four Sundays out of six. I take the pulpit two Sundays at Redwood Chapel and two Sundays at our new work in Fremont. The other two Sundays I sit in the pews and hear some tremendous Bible messages from our pastor.

"He tries to get the best out of each of us. He doesn't try to make us fit into his mold or be puppets carrying out his wishes in every detail of our activities. Oh, he knows what's going on, and if we weren't doing our jobs, we'd hear about it. We would expect to. But as long as we're concerned about the things of God, the church, and the people to whom we're striving to minister, he allows us real freedom. Personally, I feel the church is better for it.

"There's one more thing. I can't recall a single church board meeting or a staff or business meeting when I wouldn't have been happy to have an unsaved friend present. I give Pastor Williams credit for that. He doesn't dominate, and if someone expresses a view that differs from his, he doesn't act as though the fellow has denied the virgin birth or the deity of Christ.

"We sometimes do have differences of opinion. Men often express themselves frankly in opposition to some policy the pastor wants to see initiated. He doesn't back off at the first show of opposition. He will restate his case with all the persuasiveness he can command. Sometimes he loses the point, but he never raises his voice or allows opposition to ruffle his temper. He takes it in Christian love. His attitude sets the tone for our meetings. We also have a great group of lay leaders; they're really a delight to work with."

Branch Churches

Pastor Sherman Williams has long had definite convictions about the size of the ideal church. "When I came to Castro Valley," he says, "I was determined to keep the church from growing beyond 500. I was sure that was as large a congregation as one man could get to know. I felt that the ideal is a family church where the pastor could know practically all the people and minister to their needs."

Yet by 1974 Redwood Chapel had more than 850 members. How does Williams feel about that? "I've spent quite a lot of time in prayer seeking God's mind on the matter," he says. "I don't feel we would be justified in stopping our efforts to reach out and bring in those who are without Christ. But I do believe we have an obligation to start other churches. We've already done that in two cases and have plans for starting others as soon as it is practical."

In 1968, Redwood Chapel started a new congregation in Pleasanton, a nearby suburb. There were 75 or 100 people attending the Chapel who lived in that area. They would make an excellent nucleus.

"We began to sell them on the philosophy of starting a new church several months before the actual proposal was made," Williams recalls. "By that time they were prepared for it." Today the new congregation is solidly established.

Though the loss of 100 members at one time cut down on the membership and average attendance at Redwood Chapel for a time, it wasn't long until they had regained more people than they had lost and were forging ahead.

Fremont was another California community God was laying on the heart of Sherman Williams and his people. The time seemed right for them to move in that direction.

In the summer of 1973, Sherman Williams III, the aggressive 31-year-old son of Pastor Williams, was restless. He had resigned as president of Four Most Productions and sold his stock in the Illinois-based firm. Even though he was comparatively young, his experience had been varied. For several years he had served as a producer for Moody Bible Institute's radio station in Chicago, WMBI. For more than a year, he had produced "Day of Discovery," the Radio Bible Class TV program which features Richard De Haan. He had also helped found the Community Church in St. Petersburg, Fla. and Circle Church in Chicago. However, he was uncertain about the future and was seeking God's will for his life.

At about the same time, the board and staff at Redwood Chapel were praying about starting a new work at Fremont. A man to serve as pastor was the first consideration.

"We were trying to figure out how we could manage it until we got another man on the staff," Doty says. "We could handle the preaching all right. There were enough of us available for that. But we couldn't see how we could get the rest of the work done. Someone would have to do an almost endless amount of visitation, planning, organization, and administration. Then there was the matter of counseling. Who could take the time to help the people with their problems when we were all jammed tight with work?"

The only solution was to find another man who could assume most of the responsibility. With his experience and training, young Williams seemed an ideal choice. He, his wife, Marti, and their two children moved to Fremont and set to work. In the fall they had their first meeting. A few months later attendance at the new work was more than 150, with a high school group of 25 to 30.

Property has been purchased (11 acres) and building plans are under way. At this writing the young congregation is meeting in the auditorium of the Mission San Jose High School, across the street from the church property. The school's classrooms serve for their Sunday School.

As might be expected in light of his association with the St. Petersburg Community Church and Chicago's Circle Church, Sherman Williams III organized the program at Fremont on less conventional lines than at the Redwood Chapel. The worship service is first with Sunday School following. Instead of attending a regular Sunday School class, first-timers and older young people and adults may elect to attend the pastor's class, where they can discuss with him the morning message.

Williams works hard to make the service thematic. The music, the Scripture reading—all the preliminaries are built around the subject of the sermon. Sherm even goes so far as to find bulletins with a cover illustration that portrays his theme.

If Neal Doty is scheduled to speak at Fremont, he gives young Sherm his topic 10 days in advance. "I'm going to speak on the omnipotence of God next Sunday," Redwood's associate pastor says, as an example. "I'll talk about the will of God and the involvement of God in our lives. We will probably have instruction time with a response in music after each point in the message, I really enjoy it."

After the morning service, some of the people discuss the message that has just been brought. They may have questions. Some will agree with the speaker and some may disagree. It makes for some interesting Sunday School periods.

Not all the staff feel comfortable in that sort of situation. "They don't say anything about it," Doty says, "but I doubt that Pastor Williams and Pastor Miller enjoy the format at Fremont as much as Don Larmour and I do, or Sherman III. I suppose we haven't had as long to fit into a particular type of worship service. But both of the older men do go along with the Fremont approach."

On the average the people in the new congregation are comparatively young. They are attracted by the fresh, honest approach to the Gospel they have found in the Fremont Community Church.

"I first started coming here," Wayne Clark said, "when I asked a Christian neighbor about dedicating our child. I had some questions about it. I don't know whether he could have answered them or not, but he suggested that we start going to the church where he and his wife went. He said my questions would be answered there. We attended once and there was such love among the people in the congregation for us, as well as for each other, that we kept going back.

"Some churches I've gone to have preachers who seem to want to make a guy feel good. Here, I sometimes feel as though I've been tried and found guilty. Other times I feel good when I realize what God has done for me."

Paul Carroll and his family had just moved into the area and were looking for a church home. They kept seeing the Fremont Community Church sign, and when they didn't find a church home that suited them, they finally tried the little congregation.

"It took only one visit," Paul says. "The church is Spirit-filled, and that's what we were looking for. We found that the people truly do love one another."

Since Paul and his wife were a little older than the average Fremont Community Church member, he was concerned that something be done to attract a few couples over 40.

"The programming is all right," he went on, "but I don't believe it's all that important. I think it's the personal evangelism that's being done and the love the people show for each other and for newcomers who visit that sets this church apart."

Mrs. Judy Jackson, on the other hand, was repelled at first by the same features that attracted others. She was brought to the church by her sister, who was a member. She came because she was curious to see what went on there, not because she thought the church or the service offered anything for her.

"In a way I guess I liked it," she admits, "but I was so hostile I made myself believe I hated it. There wasn't one feature I would commend. I couldn't stand the friendliness of the people or the way they stuck to the Bible. And I thought it was sacrilege not to take communion every week the way they did in my church. I missed the ceremony.

"I did come to church somewhat regularly, though, before I became a Christian. It got to me that I was invited back but nobody bugged me. I soon sensed that there was a lot of love in the church which the people showed in different ways. They weren't just putting me on. They did care about me.

"It's too long a story to tell but I became a Christian. My husband has just received Christ as his Saviour, and our daughter loves the church. She discusses things with me now, when before I had to pry information out of her.

"I love coming here. I hope the church doesn't get too big. I'm afraid size would cause us to lose something that is very precious to me and my family."

Jim True and his wife also came to the church to see what was going on there. He had been introduced to evangelical Christianity by his grandmother, who took him to a church where only hell-fire and brimstone was preached. He didn't know that he ever wanted to go to another service.

"We didn't hear anything about love and we certainly didn't see it in the lives and actions of many of the people," he says.

But Jim and his wife and their two-year-old son attended Fremont Community Church a couple of times. They both thought they were Christians but soon learned that they weren't. They were only deceiving themselves. Once they got into the Word, they soon put their trust in Jesus Christ.

"I suppose the Wednesday night prayer meetings have helped me grow more than anything else," Jim says. "That's really where our understanding of the Word and love and fellowship began. We heard others get up and share what their lives had been and how Christ had changed them. I honestly felt I was betraying a trust by not becoming a Christian.

"Our church has a personality of love on a family scale. We haven't tried to reach out just to men or to women or to kids. We have reached out to the entire family. That's what makes it so great."

"Therefore, as God's chosen people, holy and dearly loved, clothe yourselves with compassion, kindness, humility, gentleness, and patience. Bear with each other and forgive whatever grievances you may have against one another. Forgive as the Lord forgave you. And over all these virtues put on love, which binds them all together in perfect unity" (COL. 3:12-14).

10

The Big Picture

"Our program has been refined and adapted in the years since we came to Castro Valley in 1961," Pastor Sherman Williams says. "We've had to change in order to keep pace with the changing needs of the people we're called to reach. But our basic philosophy is still the same. The entire ministry is founded on the principle of a TOTAL CHURCH PRO-GRAM. We strive to provide something for everyone—from the nursery for babies and small children to a program of out-reach and help for senior citizens."

Like most churches, Redwood Chapel thought it *had* a total program before a complete analysis was made and goals were adopted. They had a cradle roll, Sunday School with a full range of classes, a youth department, women's organizations, and outreach through missionaries they supported. Add those elements to a strong Bible-preaching pulpit ministry and the program was all there. Yet, as Williams guided lay leaders into a penetrating analysis of what they were doing they saw two defects: (1) there were gaping holes in their ministry, and (2) there was an uneven emphasis on certain departments.

"I had the advantage of years of experience with one of the foremost Sunday School publishing houses in the country," Williams explains, "so I had seen, first hand, many of the difficulties. Still, I was surprised at some of the problems our analysis uncovered."

Settle on Broad Goals

"If I were advising any pastor or church board who planned to establish a Total Program," says Williams, "I would urge them to set down their broad goals on paper. What is their purpose in existing? What do they hope to accomplish?"

A survey group might come up with the following general goals or purposes:

We want to reach the lost in our community for Jesus Christ.

We want to meet the needs of believers and help them find the answers to their problems.

We want to help Christians strengthen their faith in Christ and make Him a vital force in every area of their lives.

Once those purposes are worked out, the church program can be analyzed and weighed against one or another of the goals. "You might find that much of what you are doing doesn't contribute to any of them," he says. "You may be going overboard on social activities, for example. Some fine evangelical churches do just that. Or, you may be long on what I would term Christian entertainment. Some churches have a parade of soloists and singing groups with no more purpose than to bring in large crowds.

"I'm not opposed to people who go around the country appearing in churches. Many of them have a tremendous ministry both to unbelievers and to Christians. I'm talking about imbalance, about bringing in so many guests that there isn't time for solid Bible preaching on Sunday nights. These things all have to be weighed to learn their value. Goals give us an accurate scale for such an assessment."

When the church has accurately assessed its program, the staff and board are ready to consider the areas that need changes, strengthening, or additions. If the analysis and evaluation has been done accurately, the task of pin-pointing trouble spots is greatly simplified.

"I think a good example of that," Neal Doty relates, "is our nursery. It was established to meet a particular need.

"The men saw that we weren't adequately serving the young couples with small children. We didn't have as many attending our services as we should have had; the attendance of some of those who did come was inconsistent; and the problem of caring for a youngster or two during church kept young parents from getting the full impact of the messages.

"We looked behind the facts that young parents were not attending church as regularly as they should to the real reason. Caring for their children during church was so bothersome they were coming infrequently or not at all. So a top-quality nursery was set up.

"Like everything else Redwood Chapel does, the nursery was well planned and sharply operated. It was specifically designed to care for the needs of small children—to make their church attendance a happy experience. Many young couples, after attending other churches without a good nursery, have commented that their children had hated to go to church, and had cried when they got ready to leave home for church. Now some grateful young fathers and mothers say their children cry when it it time to leave church for home!

"The nursery is not only a quality facility, but the personnel who help with it are chosen because of their genuine love for children, and they are adequately trained. They know how to make their young charges feel loved and appreciated. I should know. My mother heads the staff.

"More important, the nursery has fulfilled the purpose for which it was organized. More young parents are attending the services and taking an active part in the church. When some of those young parents receive Christ, the women in the nursery can know they contributed to bringing about those decisions."

Establish Specific Short-term Goals
Once church leaders begin to put a program into effect, they should establish specific goals. For example:

"By the end of two years we plan to have every Sunday School teacher complete our teacher-training program.

By this time next year we will have established an adequate nursery.

Before the next annual meeting we will have increased our missionary giving by 20%.

"Such goals are definite," Williams says, "and measurable. You can check up on yourself periodically to see how well you are doing."

The people at Redwood Chapel discovered, soon after putting the Total Church Program into effect, that it multiplied the outreach of the church. A woman who starts attending a Bible study may get her children started in Sunday School and one of the Boys or Girls Clubs. Eventually the entire family may receive Christ and come into the membership and full fellowship of the church.

"We've seen that happen in the case of every department," Pastor Williams says. "We've had parents enroll their daughter in the Redwood Christian day school because they were concerned about conditions in their particular public school. The girl hears about the choir we have for kids her age and starts singing in it. This draws her into Sunday School. The first thing we know she has her parents at a Sunday evening service to hear her sing. We've seen mothers and fathers and several brothers and sisters reached for Christ because one of their number got interested in one phase of our program.

"We've had entire families brought to a saving knowledge of Christ because one person turned on his radio or TV Channel 12B and caught 'Sunday Nite Sing' or one of the other Gospel programs."

Adapt the Program to the People

Everyone associated with Redwood Chapel is excited about the fact that there are so many opportunities to reach the lost for Christ through their TOTAL CHURCH PROGRAM. However, Pastor Williams is quick to point out the fallacy of trying to transplant their program into another situation.

"I wouldn't advise anyone to try that," he says, "with our program or that of any other church, no matter how successful. Any program must be tailored to the needs of the people if it is to be effective."

A church in a New York suburb where most of the men are executives with heavy responsibilities would have a difficult time getting those same men to come out to an evening Bible study. In a rural community or a small town the men might look forward to such an opportunity to get together.

In some areas visitation pays huge dividends in increasing the effectiveness and outreach of the church. In another the home owners have sought a particular suburb because of regulations that require houses to be built on two-acre plots. For one reason or another the people want seclusion. A visitation program in such an area could be frowned on as an invasion of privacy and actually be harmful. A home Bible study group could better serve to reach them.

The Bible study for the wives of alcoholic husbands was established to meet a specific need. The Halloween parties, so effective in bringing in kids who have never before been interested in anything Christian, were set up to take advantage of the average high schooler's desire for fun and excitement. The television programs present fine music and challenging messages designed to interest those who are outside of Christ.

"Any given program we have may or may not be successful in another situation," Williams says. "It depends entirely on the needs of the people and the abilities and the training of those charged with putting it into effect."

"By All Means, Communicate"

Though no one involved in revamping the program at Redwood Chapel, including Pastor Williams, foresaw the broadening effect the TOTAL CHURCH PROGRAM would have on the congregation, it has given the people open minds toward Christian efforts outside their local church.

" 'By All Means, Communicate' is more than a motto at Redwood," Neal Doty says. "Many churches become so wrapped up in their own activities that they become self-centered or ingrown. It is difficult to get them to participate in activities that involve the whole Christian community. Redwood Chapel, however, is extremely active not only in participating but in initiating community-wide ministries.

"Pastor Williams was responsible for starting the Bay Area Sunday School Association, and has been active in it since its inception. With the blessing of the church he also serves on the board of the National Association of Evangelicals, and has been president of the National Sunday School Association.

"Leadership Training Institutes are held yearly. These involve not only Redwood people but folks from many smaller churches. They come because they are interested in discovering and developing spiritual gifts for spiritual service. And we are interested in helping them.

"The television ministry is a good example of 'By All Means, Communicate!' The goal of our TV work has never been to bring people into Redwood Chapel—though that happens. Our purpose is to minister to people in the community through television by reaching them where they are."

Pastor Williams sums it all up. "Program is important. So are sound preaching and a dedicated, well-trained staff. We need a TOTAL CHURCH PROGRAM. Every church does. But I think that young man in the Fremont church, Jim True, put his finger on the key to lasting success. Jim says, 'Love is the thing that puts it all together. Love is what makes our church so great.' The love of Christ showing through the members of the congregation to each other and those outside of Christ is a beacon light to lonely hearts in a desolate, unfriendly world of darkness and sin.

"If I were to leave one last bit of advice to the church considering a TOTAL CHURCH PROGRAM I would say, 'By all means put it into effect just as soon as you can, but remember, it is no substitute for love!' "

"And now I will show you the most excellent way. . . . Love never fails" (1 COR. 12:31; 13:8).

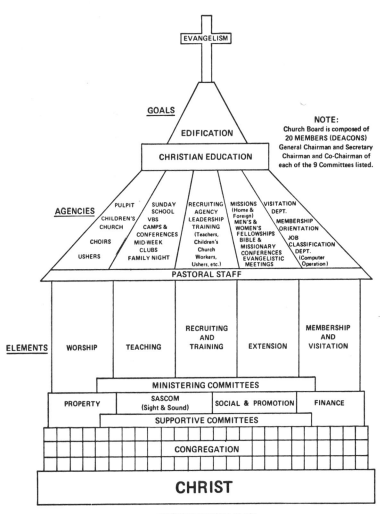

EVANGELISM

GOALS

EDIFICATION

CHRISTIAN EDUCATION

NOTE:
Church Board is composed of
20 MEMBERS (DEACONS)
General Chairman and Secretary
Chairman and Co-Chairman of
each of the 9 Committees listed.

AGENCIES

PULPIT

CHILDREN'S CHURCH

CHOIRS

USHERS

SUNDAY SCHOOL
VBS
CAMPS & CONFERENCES
MID-WEEK CLUBS
FAMILY NIGHT

RECRUITING AGENCY
LEADERSHIP TRAINING
(Teachers, Children's Church Workers, Ushers, etc.)

MISSIONS (Home & Foreign)
MEN'S & WOMEN'S FELLOWSHIPS
BIBLE & MISSIONARY CONFERENCES
EVANGELISTIC MEETINGS

VISITATION DEPT.
MEMBERSHIP ORIENTATION
JOB CLASSIFICATION DEPT.
(Computer Operation)

PASTORAL STAFF

ELEMENTS

| WORSHIP | TEACHING | RECRUITING AND TRAINING | EXTENSION | MEMBERSHIP AND VISITATION |

MINISTERING COMMITTEES

| PROPERTY | SASCOM (Sight & Sound) | SOCIAL & PROMOTION | FINANCE |

SUPPORTIVE COMMITTEES

CONGREGATION

CHRIST

ORGANIZATIONAL PLAN
REDWOOD CHAPEL COMMUNITY CHURCH

REDWOOD CHAPEL Materials Available

Packet 1 $1

Church Constitution
Membership Application
Privilege and Responsibility Questionnaire
Christian Worker's Profile
Evaluation Questionnaires for Sunday School,
    Children's Church, and Family Nite Workers
Summary Report Forms
Sunday School Report Cards
Promotional Samples

Packet 2 $4

Sunday School Worker's Guidebook
Children's Church Worker's Guidebook
Family Nite Worker's Guidebook
Discussion Leader's Guide
Sunday School Secretary's Manual
    plus all materials in packet 1

Order from:
                Redwood Chapel Community Church
                19300 Redwood Road
                Castro Valley, California 94546

Index